# MASTER YOUR NEXT MOVE

# THE NEXT STEP FORWARD

D1616302

## Thread With Purpose and Meaning

### Sherman Bush

# Table of Contents

# Chapter 1:

# Visualise Your Success In Life

When you have a clear idea of what you want in life, it becomes easier to achieve somehow. When you visualize yourself doing something, you automatically tend to get the results better. You can imagine your success in your mind before you even reach it so that it gives you a sense of comfort. You get the confidence that you can do whatever you desire. You complete your task more quickly because you have already done it once in your mind before even starting it. It relaxes us so we can interpret the outcome. You dream about your goals and remind yourself almost every day what you genuinely want or need. You become goal-oriented just by imagining your outcomes and results. Your brain tends to provide you with every possible option of opportunity you can have by visualizing. By this, you can take your dreams and desire into the real world and achieve them by knowing the possible outcome already.

Everyone today wants their picture-perfect life. They are derived from working for it, and they even manage to achieve it sometimes. People love the success which they had already estimated to happen one day. They knew they would be successful because they not only worked for it but, they also visualized it in their brains. Everything eventually falls into place once you remind yourself of your goals constantly and sometimes write it into a few words. Writing your goals down helps you immensely.

It is the idea of a constant reminder for you. So, now whenever you look on that paper or note, you find yourself recognizing your path towards success. That is one of the ways you could visualize yourself as a successful person in the coming era.

Another way to visualize your success is through private dialogue. One has to talk its way through success. It's a meaningful way to know your heart's content and what it is you are looking for in this whole dilemma. You can then easily interpret your thoughts into words. It becomes easier to tell people what you want. It is an essential factor to choose between something. Weighing your options, analyzing every detail, and you get your answer. It requires planning for every big event ahead and those to come. You ready yourself for such things beforehand so that you will know the result.

Every single goal of yours will count. So, we have to make sure that we give our attention to short-term goals and long-term goals. We have to take in the details, not leaving anything behind in the way or so. We have to make sure that everything we do is considered by ourselves first. Short-term goals are necessary for you to achieve small incomes, giving you a sense of pride. Long-term plans are more time-consuming, and it takes a lot of hard work and patience from a person. Visualizing a long-term goal might be a risk, something as big as a long-term achievement can have loads of different outcomes, and we may get distracted from our goal to become successful in life. But, visualizing does help you work correctly to get to know what will be your next step. You can make schemes in your mind about specific projects and how to work them out. Those scheming will help you in your present and future. So, it is essential to look at every small detail and imagine short-term goals and long-term goals.

Visualizing your success creates creative ideas in your mind. Your mind gets used to imagining things like these, and it automatically processes the whole plan in your mind. You then start to get more ideas and opportunities in life. You just need to close your eyes and imagine whatever you need to in as vivid detail as possible. Almost everything done by you is a result of thoughts of your mind. It is like another person living inside of you, who tells you what to do. It asks you to be alert and move. It also means the result of the possible outcome of a situation. Every action of you is your mind. Every word you speak is your mind talking.

## Chapter 2:

# How To Tell It's Time To Move On

# From Your Job Or Switch Careers

Making the decision to move on from your job is never easy. However, if you're a skilled professional who's looking for a new role, there's a vast range of opportunities available, and the team at Huxley are here to help you. We took a look at some of the key signs that could suggest it's time for you to seriously start considering your options.

You work to live, you don't live to work. While most jobs will involve the occasional late night in the office, if you're constantly starting work at seven in the morning, and not leaving until eight at night, it could be time to re-evaluate.

You work hard so you can enjoy a lifestyle you deserve. And if you don't feel you're being paid fairly, it's time to look elsewhere and find a company that will value your worth. We can give you access to a range of positions with competitive salaries across IT, Engineering, Energy, and Banking and Finance.

The biggest reason people leave their job is due to a lack of opportunities for progression. Staying in a job for too long with no development isn't only de-motivating, it can also leave hiring managers questioning your credibility. Perhaps you're seeing others getting promoted around you? Or, more worryingly, is there a distinct lack of progression within your team? If alarm bells are ringing, it's probably time to check out, and move somewhere you'll really be appreciated.

Some people go to work, do their job, and go home. And that's fine. But do you ever find yourself wishing you were more involved in a team? Or shared similar values to your organisation? If so, maybe the culture of your company isn't right for you. At Huxley, our consultants work hard to learn as much as possible about you. This allows us to not just to match you with the right job, but to find a company and team that are right for you.

For ambitious professionals, personal growth and development is extremely important. If you feel like you've learned everything you can within your role, then it's probably time to move on. Your job should challenge, motivate, and offer you the opportunity to continuously learn new skills. At Huxley, we have a range of roles available with companies of all sizes that offer a variety of development programmes to ensure you're constantly learning, and getting something extra out of your job.

When all is said and done, if the time has come to move on – you'll know. Just as there's no perfect timing, there's no right or wrong reason for quitting your job. You know yourself better than anyone else. And if you're ready to go, we're here for you.

Whatever your reasons for wanting to make a move, Huxley are here to help. Our dedicated consultants are on hand to offer personalised advice, and work in partnership with all candidates we place. By gaining a comprehensive understanding of your needs and desires, we can find a job that offers the career satisfaction you deserve.

# Chapter 3:

# How To Find Your Passion

Today we're going to talk about a topic that i think many of you are interested to know about. And that is how to find your passion.

For many of us, the realities of work and obligations means that we end up doing something we dislike for the money in the hopes that it might buy us some happiness. That sometimes we stop following our passion because maybe it does not exactly pay very well. And that is a fair decision to make.

But today, i hope to be able to help you follow at least one passion project at any point in your life in the hopes that it might help elevate your spirits, give your life more meaning, and help you live each day with a renewed drive and purpose.

You see, the world can be very dull if we chase something that we actually don't really feel attracted to. For example, when we are forced to do something out of sheer dread day in and day out, it will suck the living soul out of us and we will tend to fall into the trap of running an endless wheel with no hope in sight. When we chase material things for example, money or luxury products, we sell our soul to a job that pays well physically but not emotionally and spiritually. As a human being, we have traded our very essence and time, for a piece of paper or digital currency that serves no purpose than to enrich us externally. While it might feel good to be living comfortably, past a certain threshold, there is a point of diminishing returns. And more money just doesn't bring you that much joy anymore.

Yes you may have the fanciest, car, house, and whatever physical possessions you have. But how many of you have heard stories of people who have a lot of money but end up depressed, or end up blowing it all away because they can never spend enough to satisfy their cravings for physical goods and services. What these people lacked in emotional growth, they tried to overcompensate with money. And as their inner self gets emptier and emptier, they themselves get poorer and poorer as well.

On the flip side, many would argue that passion is overrated. That passion is nothing but some imaginary thing that we tell ourselves we need to have in order to be happy. But i am here to argue that you do not need to make passion your career in order to be happy.

You see, passion is an aspiration, passion is something that excites you, passion is something that you would do even if it does not pay a single cent. That you would gladly trade your time readily for even if it meant u weren't getting anything monetary in return. Because this passion unlocks something within you that cannot be explained with being awarded physical prizes. It is the feeling that you are truly alive and happy, you are so incredibly grateful and thankful to be doing at that very moment in time, that nothing else mattered, not even sleep.

To me, and I hope you will see this too, that passion can be anything you make it out to be. It can be something as simple as a passion for singing, a passion for creating music, a passion for helping others, passion for supporting your family, passion for starting a family, passion for doing charity work, passion for supporting a cause monetarily, or even a passion for living life to the fullest and being grateful each day.

For some lucky ones, they have managed to marry their passion with their career. They have somehow made their favourite thing to do their job, and it fulfills them each day. To those people, i congratulate you and envy you.

But for the rest of us, our passion can be something we align our soul with as long as it fulfils us as well. If we have multiple mouths to feed, we can make our passion as being the breadwinner to provide for our family if it brings us joy to see them happy. If we have a day job that we hate but can't let go off for whatever reasons, we can have a passion for helping others, to use the income that we make to better the lives of others.

And for those who have free time but are not sure what to do with it, to just simply start exploring different interests and see what hobbies you resonate with. You may never know what you might discover if you did a little digging.

What I have come to realize is that passions rarely stay the same. They change as we change, they evolve over time just as we grow. And many of the passions we had when we were younger, we might outgrow them when we hit a certain age. As our priorities in life change, our passions follow along.

In my opinion, you do not need to make your passion your career in order to be truly happy.. I believe that all you need is to have at least 1 passion project at any given point of time in your life to sustain you emotionally and spiritually. Something that you can look forward to on your off days, in your time away from work, that you can pour all your time and energy into willingly without feeling that you have wasted any second. And who knows, you might feel so strongly about that passion project that you might even decide to make it your career some day. The thing is you never really know. Life is mysterious like that.

All I do know is that chasing money for the wrong reasons will never net u happiness. But having a passion, whatever it may be, will keep you grounded and alive.

So I challenge each and everyone of you today to look into your current life, and see there are any bright spots that you have neglected that you could revive and make it your passion project. Remember that passion can be anything you make out to be as long as you derive fulfilment and happiness from it. Helpfully one that isnt material or monetary.

## Chapter 4:

# 7 Ways To Discover Your Strengths

It is a fact that everybody has at least one skill, one talent, and one gift that is unique to them only. Everyone has their own set of strengths and weaknesses. Helen Keller was blind but her talent of speaking moved the world. Stephen Hawking theorised the genesis by sitting paralyzed in a wheelchair. The barber who does your hair must have a gifted hand for setting YOUR hair at reasonable prices—otherwise you wouldn't be visiting them.

See, the thing is, everyone is a prodigy at one thing or another. It's only waiting to be discovered and harnessed. Keeping that fact in mind...

Here are 7 Ways You can Discover Your Potential Strengths and Change Your Life Forever:

1. Try Doing Things That You Have Never Done

Imagine what would have happened if Elvis Presley never tried singing, if Michael Jordan never tried playing basketball or if Mark Zuckerberg never tried coding. These individuals would have been completely different persons, serving different purposes in life. Even the whole world would've been different today if some specific people didn't try doing some specific things in their lives.

Unfortunately, many of us never get to know what we are truly good at only because we don't choose to do new things. We don't feel the need to try and explore things that we have never done before in our lives. As a result, our gifted talents remain undiscovered and many of us die with it. So while the time is high, do as many different things you can and see what suits you naturally. That is how you can discover your talent and afterwards, it's only a matter of time before you put it to good use and see your life change dramatically.

## 2. Don't Get Too Comfortable With Your Current State

It is often the case that we cling on to our current state of being and feel absolutely comfortable in doing so. In some cases, people may even embrace the job that they don't like doing only because 'it pays enough'. And honestly, I totally respect their point of view, it's up to people what makes them happy. But if you ask me how one can discover their hidden talents—how one might distinguish oneself—then I'm going to have to say that never get used to doing one particular thing. If one job or activity occupies you so much that you can't even think of something else, then you can never go out to venture about doing new stuff. The key is to get out, or should I say 'break out' from what you are doing right now and move on to the next thing. What is the next thing you might want to try doing before you die? Life is short, you don't want to go on your whole life, never having experienced something out of your comfort bubble.

## 3. What Is The Easiest Thing You Can Do?

Have you ever found yourself in a place where you did something for the first time and immediately you stood out from the others? If yes, then chances are, that thing might be one of your natural strengths.

If you've seen 'Forrest Gump', you should remember the scene where Forrest plays table-tennis for the first time in a hospital and he's just perfect at the game. "For some reason, ping-pong came very naturally to me, so I started playing it all the time. I played ping-pong even when I didn't have anyone to play ping-pong with.", says Forrest in the movie.

So bottomline, pay attention to it if something comes about being 'too easy' for you. Who knows, you might be the world's best at it.

### 4. Take Self-Assessment Tests

There are countless, free self-assessment tests that are available online in all different kinds of formats. Just google it and take as many tests you like. Some of these are just plain and general aptitude tests or IQ tests, personality tests etc. while there are others which are more particular and tell you what type of job is suited for you, what kind of skills you might have, what you might be good at, and those kinds of things. These tests are nothing but a number of carefully scripted questions which reveal a certain result based on how you answered each question. A typical quiz wouldn't take more than 30 minutes while there are some short and long quizzes which might take 15 minutes and 45 minutes respectively.

Though the results are not very accurate, it can do a pretty good job at giving you a comprehensive, shallow idea of who you are and what you can be good at.

### 5. Make Notes On How You Deal With Your Problems

Everyone faces difficult situations and overcomes them in one way or the other. That's just life. You have problems, you deal with them, you move on and repeat.

But trouble comes in all shapes and sizes and with that, you are forced to explore your problem-solving skills—you change your strategies and tactics—and while at it, sometimes you do things that are extraordinary for you, without even realizing it. John Pemberton was trying out a way to solve his headache problem using Coca leaves and Kola nuts, but incidentally he made the world's coke-drink without even knowing about it. Lesson to be learned, see how YOU deal with certain problems and why is it different from the others who are trying to solve the same problem as you.

### 6. Ask Your Closest Friends and Family

People who spend a lot of time with you, whether it be your friend, family or even a colleague gets to see you closely, how you work, how you behave, how you function overall. They know what kind of a person you are and at one point, they can see through you in a manner that you yourself never can. So, go ahead and talk to them, ask them what THEY think your strongest suit can be—listen to them, try doing what they think you might turn out to be really good at, Who knows?

7. Challenge Yourself

The growth of a human being directly corresponds to the amount of challenge a person faces from time to time. The more a person struggles, the more he or she grows—unlocks newer sets of skills and strengths. This is a lifelong process and there's no limit on how far you can go, how high your talents can accomplish.

Now, one might say, "what if I don't have to struggle too much? What if my life is going easy on me?". For them, I'd say "invite trouble". Because if you are eager to know about your skills and strengths (I assume you are since you're reading this), you must make yourself face difficulties and grow from those experiences. Each challenge you encounter and overcome redefines your total strength.

Final Thoughts

To sum it up, your life is in your hands, under your control. But life is short and you gotta move fast. Stop pursuing what you are not supposed to do and set out to find your natural talents RIGHT NOW. Once you get to know your strengths, you will have met your purpose in life.

# Chapter 5:

# Enjoying The Journey

Today I want to talk about why enjoying the journey of life is important. And why hurrying to get to the destination might not be all that enjoyable as we think it is.

A lot of us plan our lives around an end goal, whether it be getting to a particular position in our company's ladder, or becoming the best player in a sport, or having the most followers on Instagram or whatever the goal may be... Many of us just can't wait to get there. However, many a times, once we reach our goal, whilst we may feel a sense of satisfaction and accomplishment for a brief moment, we inevitably feel like something is missing again and we search for our next objective and target to hit.

I have come to realise that in life, it is not always so much the end goal, but the journey, trials, struggles, and tribulations that make the journey there worth it. If we only focus on the end goal, we may miss out the amazing sights along the way. We will ultimately miss the point of the journey and why we embarked on it in the first place.

Athletes who achieve one major title never stop at just that one, they look for the next milestone they can achieve, but they enjoy the process, they take it one step at a time and at the end of their careers they can look back with joy that they had left no stone unturned. And that they can live their life without regret.

How many times have you seen celebrities winning the biggest prize in their careers, whether it may be the Grammy's Album of the Year if you are a musician, or the Oscars Best Actor or Best Actress Award. How many of them actually feel like that is the end of the journey? They keep creating and keep making movies and film not because they want that award, even though it is certainly a nice distinction to have, but more so because they enjoy their craft and they enjoy the art of producing.

If winning that trophy was the end goal, we would see many artists just end their careers there and then after reaching the summit. However that is not the case. They will try to create something new for as long as people are engaged with their craft, as with the case of Meryl Streep, even at 70+ she is still working her butt off even after she has achieve all the fame and money in the world.

Even for myself, at times i just want to reach the end as quickly as possible. But many times when i get there, i am never satisfied. I feel empty inside and i feel that I should be doing more. And when i rush to the end, i do feel like I missed many important sights along the way that would have made the journey much more rewarding and enjoyable had I told myself to slow it down just a little.

I believe that for all of us, the journey is much more important than the destination. It is through the journey that we grow as a person, it is through the journey that we evolve and take on new ideas, work ethics, knowledge, and many little nuggets that make the trip worth it at the end. If someone were to hand you a grand slam title without having you earned it, it would be an empty trophy with no meaning and emotions behind it. The trophy would not represent the hours of hard work that you have put in to be deserving of that title.

So I challenge each and everyone of you today to take a step back in whatever journey you may be on. To analyse in what aspects can you enjoy the moment and to not place so much pressure into getting to the destination asap. Take it one day at a time and see how the journey you are on is actually a meaningful one that you should treasure each day and not let up.

# Chapter 6:

# Change Your Environment For Success

Human life resembles a lot of things. Take leaves of a tree for example. Leaves change color throughout the year. Ever thought why does it happen?

Trees change the color of their leaves to adapt to the different seasons, preparing for what is coming ahead of them.

It is not exclusive only to plants. A lot of animals also have different approaches towards different climatic changes. A lot of polar birds migrate thousands of miles due South, just before the winter season comes in. A lot of fish move to warm waters in the fall season.

Ever wondered why? Because they want o make sure the survival of their species and they want to provide a habitat for their of-springs where they can flourish and nourish well.

Do you want to be a successful human being? You should make a stronger network with your species. The more you interact with your species the more you are to have a better social life, the better chances you have at learning, and the better chances of survival you have if you have someone dependable to rely on.

The effects your environment and your company have on you will determine how pessimistic, ambitious, and or organized you are. You will feel the change in the course of events just as you start to make a change in your environment.

Every man needs a productive and nourishing environment to flourish to his or her full limits. And maybe even push the limits further.

You also need to realize that whatever you are in search of will always be achievable, but you have to make a routine and a habitat where you can relax when you are feeling low.

Most of us take our health for granted. We take our sleep for granted and a disruptive sleep cycle can change our behavior. If you don't have a good place to sleep and if you don't have a nice comfortable bed or bedding to curl up in, you will not be able to restore all your creative juices.

These juices will only flow when you will let them, and for that, you need to create a window of the calming and soothing environment to sleep in.

Now if you have a goal and you know the right path to it, stay put and start by bringing in the most relevant things nearer to you. Start pushing the unnecessary thins out of your habitat and you will be forwarding one step closer to success.

We don't realize this fully but we are truly a product of our environment and our relationships.

Every new day is a new chance to bring a change in our lives. Find new things that inspire you. Find New people that motivate you. Find newer things that push you. Find better goals that make you shine bigger and better than everyone else around you.

If you are willing to change what you love the most around you, you are already far ahead on your path to success.

## Chapter 7:

# _Successful People Start Before They Feel Ready_

We all have humble beginnings. We all start from the womb of our mothers, living the same baby life everyone else has lived before us, and everyone after us will.

We get our lives as our parents serve them to us. They send us to get the education and sometimes we have to make those arrangements for ourselves. Sometimes we get the food hot and good-looking just being served to us without even wanting to ask for it.

But life isn't always this kind and caring.

How many times do we wish for things like I will do this better tomorrow, I will get that someday, I have to look for a better job, I have to do something about the extra weight that I am carrying.

We all have a wish list and it is always growing. But rarely do we do something about them. We always go back to our normal life and don't do anything about it as we always have. Sounds familiar?

It is the reality and the curse of living in this time of having everything we can wish so never wanting to struggle for other things.

There might be a lot of reasons for every one of us for not trying, or trying but not getting what we want.

We lag in a lot of things and there are hundreds of explanations for them, but the most common is the 'FEAR'.

Fear of rejection, fear of waiting, fear of not being good enough, fear of the unknown, and mostly fear of starting something from scratch. All these fears are legitimate and justifiable, but you are not getting much by fear either. So why not be fearless and actually start doing something?

We have a lot on our plate and we all have our bad days, but to start fresh, you don't need fear or an indicator or vision, you just need the tiniest of motivation that you have to make something for yourself and you and only you are your sole driving force.

Things will start happening for you one time or the other. You only need to maintain vigor at any age you are.

You don't have a set path. Don't think that you will get mature and stable once you hit the 30's or middle age. Time will not set the path for you. You, yourself have to set the time straight.

You don't need to be 30 to be mature, you can be 15 and still be a much mature and emotionally stable person than the one who has 5 children.

Your life is in your hands and you have a responsibility towards yourself from the time you get a hold of your senses. Because you are always ready to turn things around.

You don't need to feel ready, but you need to show yourself that you were ready all along by just jumping into the pond of opportunities and the world will open its treasury for you.

You don't need to be perfect to start, but you need to start to be perfect!

**Chapter 8:**

# 6 Ways To Attract Your Potential

Do you sometimes feel like you're wasting your potential? And do you also feel unsure about how you can even reach your full potential? If so, you're like any other ambitious person who wants to make the best of his/her life. Because to me, that's what "reaching your potential" means.

We all have limited time on our hands. Some live longer than others. But you and I both know that it's not about how *long* you live, it's about *what you do* with the time you're alive. It's about leaving everything on the table and making sure you live up to your inner drive. Look, when I talk about reaching your potential, I'm not talking about what other people or society thinks we should do with our lives.

When you chase empty goals and objects, you become restless. Instead, chase your *own* potential and forget about everything external. Become the best person you can be. That's the only honourable aim there is. We identified 6 skills that will help you achieve your full potential. Here they are.

## 1. Self-Awareness

You must be comfortable with who you are and what you are. Don't try to be something you're not. And don't try to change yourself just because others tell you to. Instead, know who you are. And if you don't know, find out. Read, write, think, talk. That's self-awareness: It only requires you to be aware of your thoughts. And when you're self-aware, you automatically learn more about who you are—which is called self-knowledge. But it all starts with being aware. No awareness? No knowledge.

## 2. Leadership

First, focus on yourself. Fix your own problems. Become a stable person who you can rely on. When you do that, focus on inspiring others to do the same. The best way to help others is to teach them to rely on themselves. Sick and narcissistic people want to make people dependent on them. Leaders teach others to be independent. How? By setting a good example. There's no better way to lead.

## 3. Writing

Better writing leads to better thinking. And better thinking leads to better communication. Better communication leads to better results in your career. "What?! I never thought the writing was that important!" When you get good at one thing, it will help you to get better at other things. You see? It was only when I started writing that everything "clicked." When you become a better writer, you can easily express yourself and start making connections. That will improve your career in ways you never imagine.

## 4. Mindfulness

My definition of mindfulness might be different than yours. To be clear, I'm not talking about meditation, yoga, or Zen Buddhism. I'm talking about being a calm and mindful person. A person who's in control of their thoughts and emotions. A person who's solid as a rock. A person who others can rely on. But achieving that inner peace requires much training. I don't think we can ever fully master this skill. But by practicing control over our thoughts, we can get better. My favourite way to become more mindful is to be present. The more I *stay* in the present moment, the more mindful I am. The aim is never to be lost in thoughts. It's to be here.

## 5. Productivity

The funny thing about mindfulness is that people assume living in the present removes your drive to achieve your goals. The reverse is true. The more present I am, the more desire I feel to improve my life. And how do you improve your life? You already know it. I don't have to tell you that work is the only way to achieve things. Thinking about achieving your goals will not do anything real for you. Become a person who's productive *every day*. Make use of your time. Don't just waste it on watching tv, hanging out with your friends, gaming, or any other mindless routine activity. Know how to get the most results in the least amount of time. That's the ultimate aim of productivity skills.

# 6. Excellence

I half-assed many things in my life. "Let's just get it over with," was my motto. I was so <u>impatient</u> that I hardly did anything well. I just put in the minimum effort. Hence, I was never the best at anything. But then I realized that excellence is a skill. Look at Robert Greene who took 6 years to write another book. Or Lebron James who worked out during every off-season of his career. Or Helen Keller who published 5 books, despite being deaf and blind. But this is also true for successes that don't get attention in the media. Look at the top salesperson in any given organization who arrives early and leaves late every day. Or the mother who sacrifices nights out and dinner parties to raise her kid with all of her attention and love. That's called excellence.

**Chapter 9:**

# 8 Habits That Help You Live Longer

Habits define who you are. Each habit influences your life on a positive and negative dimensions. After all, smoking a cigarette is a habit, and so are long hours of jogging. The behaviors that negative you from attaining your full potential also shorten your life.

Exercising, consuming nutritious meals, meditating, among others, makes our lives better in immeasurable ways. Our habits take over as an autopilot when our physical and mental abilities ebb and flow with age. This is especially true if you are old enough to understand the importance of habits but still young enough to make your positive habits count. As you get older, you'll find yourself relying more and more on your habits. Create good habits, and they will serve as the autopilot on which you will trust to stay healthy, active, and engaged.

As you create and stick to that habit you love, keep longevity and quality life your ultimate goal. Even if you've had bad habits in the past, now is the moment to break them.

Here are 8 habits that could help you live a longer life.

## 1. Exercise Regularly.

Studies show that frequent, intense exercising is essential for age and physical health preservation. Getting out of your comfort zone to engage in a challenging exercise will reap benefits in the long haul. Hopping on a treadmill at a snail-like pace will do you no good. Therefore, it would help if you stalled rigorous aerobic exercises, stretching to your habit menu.

The less flexible you are, the more likely you will trip, break your hip, and end up in a nursing home like Aunt Karen. Vigorous exercise and stretching your body are the best ways to protect yourself from preventable injuries and the physical ailments of aging.

## 2. Mind Training

Mind training is equally vital as body exercises as you become older. As you train your body, your mind also needs activity to stay in good form. Learn and challenge yourself to remain alert and possibly avoid dementia. There are many mind training exercises such as puzzles, or even Sudoku, or any mind-challenging tasks.

According to a recent study conducted by John Hopkins Medicine, staying in school longer reduces the prevalence of dementia in the United States, particularly among individuals aged 65 and older.

## 3. Keep a Healthy Weight.

Maintaining a healthy body means that you are cautious of what you consume. Consider the foods that enhance your physical, mental and spiritual wellbeing by avoiding calories and refined food staff. A new article in Medical News Today by Catharine Paddock, Ph.D., advocates keeping your body mass index (BMI) under 25% if possible. Keep your body weight as healthy as possible! It will impact your longevity.

## 4. Develop a Positive Mental Attitude.

Whatever your viewpoint is on your present living conditions, impact your life in the long haul. That is, your take on your current life significantly reacts with the functioning of your body and soul. Therefore, people who adopt and adjust to a positive stereotype about aging are likely to recover faster from any disability. As a result, according to a recent study published in the Journal of the American Medical Association, longevity is achieved by maintaining positive thoughts towards your current state of affairs.

## 5. Elevate Your Mood.

As we become older, depression and anxiety might become more prevalent. Do anything you can to boost your mood, whether it's through exercise or exciting mental activity. Go for walks in the park, re-enter the dating scene, or volunteer for a cause you care about – in short, do anything that makes you feel better about yourself and the world.

## 6. Maintain Your Social Contacts.

Maintaining a social connection becomes meaningful as you grow older. You don't need a considerable social network; an influential network is enough. Your family, accordingly, may be enough, but only if the members are happy and flourishing. The Inverse is very true! If you find that your social network is exceptionally negative, look for ways to create a new one.

Make friends of different ages who may have other interests than you, and keep fostering friendships you already have or may have had in the past. Remember, that person you allow in your inner circle is equally important.

# 7. Take Charge of Your Life

Rather than being a spectator, own your life. Don't just sit and watch the world pass you. Just get out and about, engage in activities that matter at every stage of your life. This means doing what a 25 or 40-year-old does to avoid mid-life crises. It can be not easy, especially in today's internet era, where we can check what other people are up to at the hour without even leaving the couch. On the other hand, sitting on the sidelines will not help you maintain excellent physical or mental health. Make sure you're not only listening to other people's experiences; get out there and make your own.

## 8. Do Something Valuable.

Having a purpose in life and living up to it is vital. The drive doesn't have to be extravagant or mid-blowing to be meaningful as most of us think. Some people find their purpose in being an outstanding grandparent, volunteering for a cause important to them, or even mastering woodworking or gardening skills. It doesn't matter what your goal is as long as you have one.

On the other hand, not having a purpose might lead to poor habits that negatively impact your longevity and mood. Consider this: if you don't have anything to do, you can end up sitting in front of the TV all day, or worse, falling into the meaningless emptiness of social media.

## Conclusion

The great news is that you don't have to take multi-vitamins or pharmaceuticals-promoted drugs to halt aging, hunger yourself, and thirst to reduce weight, or buy the latest products promising increased brain performance. According to several studies, adopting basic steps in the short term can result in longevity benefits.

# Chapter 10:

# 10 Habits of Muhammad Ali

It has been five years since the Olympic gold-medallist, three-time heavyweight champion, and American hero Muhammad Ali passed away. Ali was a boxer, social activist, and philanthropist who is universally recognized as one of the greatest boxing champions of the twentieth century, with a record of 56 wins.

He is also renowned for his courageous, fierce opposition against the Vietnam War. Ali had a colorful life, fought for personal rights in the truest sense of the concept, and left behind a boxing legacy that will be remembered for centuries to come. His life was one of the most inspiring in modern history.

Here are the ten habits of Muhammad Ali.

## 1. Adopt a Growth Attitude

According to Dr. Dweck, Muhammad Ali's outstanding boxing career had considerably more to do with his growth-oriented psyche than the commonly accepted-yet incorrect-physical talent. Regardless of how lackluster his physical attributes were; his mind-game was on the fire. Instead of lamenting on how you're not enough, focus on embracing different paths to achieving greatness.

## 2. Affirm Your Beliefs Strongly

Ali's refusal to serve in Vietnam was premised on his respect for what he believed in. "I don't have a beef with the Viet Cong," he remarked. "Why should they expect me to put on a uniform... and drop bombs and bullets on brown people... while so-called Negroes in Louisville are treated like dogs and denied basic human rights?" This sentiment elevated Ali's status from prized heavyweight boxer to renowned civil rights figure. What about you? It's as simple as that: stay true to yourself and your ideas, no matter what they are.

## 3. Confidence Is Everything

Ali's remarkable "trash" talks before the fights were everything, and his antics enraged both fighters and fans. Sure, the sheer amount of confidence he exuded bordered on arrogance. But, based on his record, it's reasonable to assume that confidence can get you a long way. Give it a try: stand tall with your head held high.

## 4. It's Never Too Serious

In his memoir, Ali said that his most desired legacy was his sense of humor, which is evident in his cocky digs at other boxers and his poetic self-promotion. Even after Parkinson's disease, he remained as sharp as ever up to his death. This demonstrates the power of humor in defying human limits and spit in the face of adversity while making yourself youthful at heart.

## 5. Give Back

When you are given a voice, it is your responsibility to use it for others' benefit. Aside from being an unmistakable advocate for civil rights, Ali demonstrated his devotion to equality and positivism by taking on a plethora of humanitarian tasks - his negotiation for the release of numerous American prisoners in Iraq in 2001 is just one example.

## 6. Be Enthusiastic About Something

Ali was passionate about more than simply boxing. He was a devout Muslim who found great personal joy in his beliefs. Ali was a brilliant boxer, but he was also a fantastic person. Be enthusiastic about your own beliefs.

## 7. Say As You Mean It

When you look up at Muhammad's videos, you'll notice his proud, booming, and roaring voice while being interviewed, giving speeches, or even "trash" talking his opponents. This doesn't mean you go yelling at everyone at work, but a little timidity won't hurt. Try it: it's not entirely drilled sergeant, but it's also not precisely librarian.

## 8. Find and Pursue Your Purpose

Just like Ali, drag yourself to the gym before or after work, be productive at work (as much as possible), and try to make the most of your day. Every morning, get up with a sense of purpose.

## 9. Take Life By Its Horns

Ali's rise started as vengeance towards his stolen bike. Then came a Golden Gloves champion, an amateur champion, an Olympic gold medalist to having a long career as a three-time world heavyweight champion. What does this tell you? That you should always be hungry for more.

## 10. Have a Higher Goal

Muhammad once said, "you have one life; it will soon be over; what you do for God is all that will last," In order to have a meaningful and satisfying life, you must fulfil a higher purpose in your life.

## Conclusion

The next time you find yourself at the crossroads between your comfort zone and unfamiliar terrain, remember these habits and imagine Muhammad Ali's heavy glove on your shoulder, softly but firmly pressing you to walk over the line.

# Chapter 11:

# Happy People Stay Present

*"Realize deeply that the present moment is all you ever have."*

According to a study, 50% of the time, we are not fully present in the moment. We are either thinking about the past or worrying about the future. These things lead to frustration, anxiety, and pain in our daily life. Each morning as soon as we wake up, we start seeking distractions. As we wake up with a clear mind, we should be grateful for a new day that we got; instead, we start looking for our phone, start going through interwebs and rush into our days. So now we are going to help you and list some of the things that will help you stay present.

**Stop Being a Slave to Your Mind:** For the next four days, let's do an exercise where you pay attention to your thoughts and see what crosses your mind. You. You will soon realize that majority of the thoughts that you have are destructive. There will be very little time to think about the present, and the majority of your thoughts would be about the past or the future. So, whenever this happens and you find yourself wandering consciously, try to bring yourself back to the present. Also, you need to remind yourself that multi-tasking is a myth and focus on one thing only.

**Tap into Your Senses:** If you mindfully tap into your senses, you will realize that it is a fantastic way of bringing more awareness into your day. Because our eyes are wide open all day, we can see, but we forget to tap into other senses such as taste, touch, or smell. But if you use these, you can feel more present and calm down if you are in a stressful situation. You might not realize this, but our senses play a huge role in manifesting our reality. For example, everything we are hearing we are touching will regularly turn into our reality. That is why we can use the power our senses have and feel more calm and present.

**Listen Closely:** Everyone loves to talk, but only a few people like to listen. People love to share their dreams, what they have accomplished and what they desire, and still, nobody seems to be listening closely.

*"When you talk, you are only repeating what you already know. But if you listen, you may learn something new."*

When you listen carefully, you will be able to charm people and at the same time learn new things and be present. Because you will be focusing on what they are saying, you will focus on the current moment. This way, you will also be able to silence your thoughts about the past and future because you will be consciously listening and focusing on what they are saying. This will also benefit your relationship in the long run because when you need an ear to listen to your problems, they will be there for you. This is a win-win situation for you, and you will improve your relationship while practising being more present.

**Chapter 12:**

# How To Become A Morning Person

Our natural sleep/wake cycles are known as our circadian rhythm, and they can vary a lot from person to person. People fall into different groups, or chronotypes, depending on whether they feel most awake and alert in the morning, in the evening or somewhere in between.

No chronotype is inherently better or worse than another. There's nothing wrong with staying up late and sleeping in. "If that schedule fits with your lifestyle and your obligations, it's not necessary to change it."

The trouble comes when your late bedtime clashes with your early morning obligations. If you're regularly getting less than the recommended seven to nine hours of sleep a night, your health and well-being can suffer.

Unfortunately, we can't pick our chronotypes. Genetics plays a part in whether you identify as a night owl or a morning lark. Still, your habits and behaviours can reinforce those natural tendencies. And those habits aren't set in stone. "By making behavioural changes, you may be able to shift your sleep schedule preferences,"

How to reset your circadian rhythm? How, exactly, do you become more of a morning person?

Shift your bedtime: Count back from the time your alarm rings, aiming for a total of seven to nine hours a night. That will be your target bedtime — eventually. If you're used to turning in well after midnight, willing yourself to suddenly fall asleep at 10:00 p.m. is sure to backfire.

Aim to go to bed 15 or 20 minutes earlier than usual for a few days. Then push it back another 15 minutes for several more days. "It's important to adjust your sleep time gradually," she says.

Make it routine: A quiet bedtime routine is key to helping you fall asleep earlier. At least an hour before lights out, dim the lights and power down your electronics. Find something soothing to do, like taking a warm bath, reading a book or listening to a (not-too-stimulating) podcast. "Give yourself time to wind down and prepare your mind for bed."

Lighten up: "Our circadian rhythms are responsive to light and dark," Exposure to bright light first thing in the morning helps you feel more alert and also helps shift your internal rhythm toward an earlier wake time.

Natural light is the best, so get outside or open your bedroom window. If you can't get outside or your room is natural light-deprived, try a light therapy lamp that mimics the spectrum of natural light.

Make mornings more pleasant: Try to schedule something to look forward to in the morning so that getting up feels like less of a slog. Perhaps a hot cup of coffee, sipped in silence, and the daily crossword puzzle. Knowing that something pleasant awaits can help you take that first, painful step out of bed.

Move your alarm clock: Hitting snooze is all too tempting, so remove that option. Try putting your alarm clock across the room, so you have to get up to turn it off.

Some apps make it even harder to sleep in, by forcing you to engage in mentally stimulating activities like solving a puzzle to stop the beeping. "Do whatever works to keep you from hitting snooze,"

**Chapter 13:**

# 10 Habits Of Intelligent People

Many habits are synonymous with intelligent people. Some are misconceptions while others are true. Here are ten habits of intelligent people:

## 1. They Are Calm

Calmness is a rare trait. The ability to compose yourself in stormy situations and rise above any provocations has not been mastered by many people. Calmness requires mental maturity to understand that you ought not to respond to everything coming your way.

Intelligent people maintain calm even when they are pushed to the wall. They know the appropriate time to respond and do not yield to pressure.

## 2. They Are Inquisitive

Intelligence makes people interrogate situations and cross-check facts. It is unwise to accept everything at face value and intelligent people have mastered the art of inquiry. Restrain yourself from embracing everything you hear because you create enmity with people you ought to befriend.

You could be a third party to a conflict you know nothing about. Intelligent people foresee such situations and cleverly evade them.

## 3. They Do Not Rush To Take Sides

Do not hastily partake in issues you are not acquainted with. Intelligent people are only observers where they are uninvited. They avoid staining themselves with blames that they know nothing about because it has the potential to damage their reputation.

Intelligent people take time to understand situations before they side with either party. This makes them finally administer justice where required and they are praised for their wisdom.

## 4. They Are Rational

Intelligent people are not extremists. They reason within an acceptable framework to arrive at conclusions. Rationality defines intelligence and the practicability of ideas. The beliefs that intelligent people hold are reasonable and actionable.

Intelligence makes one know when to stop or advance. This makes them stand out in arriving at better decisions than those who blindly pursue unrealistic goals.

## 5. They Are Problem Solvers

Intelligent people are not fault-finders but problem-solvers. It is not enough to identify a problem because nothing would have changed. Intelligence makes one see solutions in a sea of problems. This distinguishes them from those who simply fault a situation and walk away.

Intelligent people seem to have a solution to every problem. They are revered for their insights that most people lack and are seeking to offer solutions.

## 6. They Consult Widely

Intelligent people consult widely before making important decisions. They appreciate the expertise of other people more knowledgeable than them. Consulting does not make you inferior to anybody. Accommodating the views of other people is a sign of mental maturity. The consulting habit of intelligent people makes them alive to the reality around them with divergent views since people do not think similarly. Their intelligence expands with a wider scope on the thoughts of different kinds of people.

## 7. They Do Not Dismiss Their Enemies

Your enemies can successfully plot and execute your downfall if you do not act fast enough. Many people think that alienating yourself from your enemies is better because they will not have access to you.

Intelligent people keep their friends close and their enemies even closer. They do not dismiss their enemies as trivial but neutralize every attack early enough before matters get out of hand.

## 8. They Strategize Their Every Move

Intelligent people have mastered the art of strategy. Every move they make is carefully pondered upon before execution and they have anticipated every possible reaction that could arise. They take charge not to let things happen but make them happen.

Either in pursuit of perfection or to avoid conflict, intelligent people can account for every step they make. Their lives are like a game of chess – every move is to protect the King and checkmate the opponent.

## 9. They Know When To Retreat

Who understands that retreat is not cowardice better than intelligent people do? It is a powerful art of war that dupes the enemy into thinking they have won. Intelligent people are not obsessed with victory at the expense of anything else.

The unintelligent consider retreat as a defeat when it is not. They pursue their enemies endlessly while jeopardizing the gains they may have made. Intelligent people preserve their gains by retreating at the opportune time.

## 10. They Limit Their Words

Transgression abounds in a multitude of words. Intelligent people do not have a lot of meaningless talks. They stick to only important issues and address what is required head-on without beating around the bush.

Intelligent people communicate in a few words to avoid ambiguity. They are precise in what they want and pursue it.

In conclusion, these habits of intelligent people make them stand out from their peers. Intelligence could be innate or nurtured over time but all intelligent people have a majority if not all of these ten habits.

# Chapter 14:

# What Is The Meaning of Life?

The question of the meaning of life is perhaps one that we would rather not ask, for <u>fear</u> of the answer or lack thereof. Still today, many people believe that we, humankind, are the creation of a supernatural entity called God, that God had an intelligent purpose in creating us, and that this intelligent purpose is "the meaning of life".

I do not propose to rehearse the well-worn arguments for and against the existence of God, and still less to take a side. But even if God exists, and even if He had an intelligent purpose in creating us, no one really knows what this purpose might be, or that it is especially meaningful. The Second Law of Thermodynamics states that the entropy of a closed system—including the universe itself—increases up to the point at which equilibrium is reached, and God's purpose in creating us, and, indeed, all of nature, might have been no more lofty than to catalyse this process much as soil organisms catalyse the decomposition of organic matter.

If our God-given purpose is to act as super-efficient heat dissipators, then having no purpose at all is better than having this sort of purpose—because it frees us to be the authors of our purpose or purposes and so to lead truly dignified and meaningful lives. In fact, following this logic, having no purpose at all is better than having any kind of pre-determined purpose, even more traditional, uplifting ones such as serving God or improving our karma.

In short, even if God exists, and even if He had an intelligent purpose in creating us (and why should He have had?), we do not know what this purpose might be, and, whatever it might be, we would rather be able to do without it, or at least to ignore or discount it. For unless we can be free to become the authors of our own purpose or purposes, our lives may have, at worst, no purpose at all, and, at best, only some unfathomable and potentially trivial purpose that is not of our own choosing.

You might yet object that talk about the meaning of life is neither here nor there because life is merely a prelude to some form of eternal afterlife, and this, if you will, is its purpose.

But I can marshal up at least four arguments against this position:

- It is not at all clear that there is, or even can be, some form of eternal afterlife that entails the survival of the personal ego.

- Even if there were such an afterlife, living for ever is not in itself a purpose. The concept of the afterlife merely displaces the problem to one remove, begging the question: what then is the purpose of the afterlife? If the afterlife has a pre-determined purpose, again, we do not know what that is, and, whatever it is, we would rather be able to do without it.

- Reliance on an eternal afterlife not only postpones the question of life's purpose, but also dissuades or at least discourages us from determining a purpose or purposes for what may be the only life that we do have.

**Chapter 15:**

# 10 Habits of Steve Ballmer

A step to improving your business for long-term growth and profits is learning from entrepreneurs who've proven themselves the best. One case in point is Steve Ballmer, the bold, boisterous former Microsoft CEO. He left Microsoft's top management to channel his energy into owning the LA Clippers basketball club.

Ballmer is the current owner of the Los Angeles Clippers of the National Basketball Association (NBA). Forbes recently ranked him as the 11th richest person globally, with an estimated wealth of US$71.4 billion. How did he become this wealthy?

Here are 10 habits of Steve Ballmer.

## 1. Learn With a Purpose

Working with several school teams such as basketball and football teams and the school newspaper allowed Ballmer to develop positive energy, sociability, and assertiveness that would serve his success journey well. After graduating from Harvard, he started advertising for muffin and brownie mixes at protector and gamble. You need to seek unique and challenging experiences, anything different from your daily monotony, because it is from these experiences that you'll learn and improve.

## 2. Make Yourself Indispensable

Making yourself dispensable means associating well with your peers because you never know what tomorrow holds, and when they give you a chance, don't take it for granted. Ballmer's sociability and assertiveness got him close to Bill Gates during his college days, and when he needed somewhere to start his career, his friend was there. Even though he was working for his friend, he never took work for granted; instead, his dedication to work diversified Microsoft products such as the electronic game console system Xbox and the Zune family of portable media players.

## 3. Develop a Perspective

Sometimes your point of view creates opportunity, and other times you pick up opportunities gives you a chance to build a point of view. However, an opportunity is rarely enough without a distinctive perspective to shape a generic opportunity into something extraordinary. Ballmer challenged graduates at St. Louise to develop a point of view, just like Jack Dorsey, the co-founder of both Twitter and Square, in order to create opportunities for themselves.

## 4. You Can Start Small

If you want to be rich, start from somewhere, no matter how insignificant the role is. Ballmer started as an assistant to Bill Gates, where he was earning $50,000 a year. Several years later, his efforts promoted him up until he was officially named CEO, a position he stayed in until retirement. If you want to succeed in life, there is nothing wrong with starting small. Hard work, dedication, and perseverance will always get you where you want to be.

## 5.  Don't Run Your Predecessor's Shop.

Ballmer ran Bill Gate's company until Microsoft's final reorganization but lacked Gates' unique skills. As a new executive, you have two options: change your skills to meet the organization's needs or change the organization to meet your needs. Ballmer isn't a software expert and incredibly did so well, given that he ran a company built around software expertise. Ballmer would never compete with Gates, but he did eventually make changes to Microsoft that better reflected his distinct strengths.

## 6.  Be a Step Ahead

To ensure that application developers continued using Microsoft's DOS and that Microsoft remained ahead of their competitors, Ballmer pushed Microsoft to announce widows. He had noted a possible competition from Apple after they launched their interface model. If you want to be successful and wealthy, especially if you find yourself in a competitive business line, always be one step ahead of your competitors and be competent in the decisions you make.

## 7.  Let your energy drive your work

Ballmer's drive to work, managerial talent, loyalty was infectious, according to his co-workers.  He was friendly, easy-going with a loud, exuberant style. His high energy personality influenced a lot of business interactions, which eventually drove growth over the years and made him rich. The more boisterous you are, the easier you can convince investors. Your attitude and energy towards work will enable you to apply your skills and gifts more effectively.

## 8. Numbers matter

Ballmer was a mathematician; hence you can see where his obsession for numbers is rooted from. Because today's world is data-driven, the likelihood is that his talent is more valuable now than when he was Microsoft CEO. Numbers compel you to examine the measurable facts, seek reliable information, and constantly question what is essential. According to Steve, numbers define your success and failures, hence having a solid foundation for success.

## 9. Keep It Brief

While many would go extra to writing a sentence to relay information, Ballmer isn't one of them; he can say what others can't in three words. Because of his accuracy, he was able to touch more people personally. When running a large organization, being wordy is the worst because, in addition to the listener losing track, you waste time, lose the point, and may cause you to say something you didn't intend to.

## 10. Rediscover Fun

If you no longer enjoy your job, find a way to leave. Escape the prison and find a way to reclaim the smile that everyone around you remembers so fondly. As Ballmer stepped away from Microsoft toward something that appeared to be far more enjoyable, you could also find a way to put a smile back on your face.

## Conclusion

Just like Steve Ballmer, learn skills and continually work to sharpen them. Let the skills speak for you, as the better they are, the more likely opportunities will come to you.

# Chapter 16:

# 10 Stress Management Tips

Most students experience significant amounts of stress, and this stress can take a significant toll on health, happiness, and grades. For example, a study found that teens report stress levels similar to that of adults. Stress can affect health-related behaviors like sleep patterns, diet, and exercise as well, taking a larger toll. Given that nearly half of the survey respondents reported completing three hours of homework per night in addition to their full day of school work and extracurriculars, this is understandable.

## 1. Get Enough Sleep

Students, with their packed schedules, are notorious for missing sleep. Unfortunately, operating in a sleep-deprived state puts you at a distinct disadvantage. You're less productive, you may find it more difficult to learn, and you may even be a hazard behind the wheel. Don't neglect your sleep schedule. Aim to get at least 8 hours a night and take power naps when you need them.

## 2. Practice Visualization

Using guided imagery to reduce stress is easy and effective. Visualizations can help you calm down, detach from what's stressing you, and turn off your body's stress response. You can also use visualizations to prepare for presentations and score higher on tests by vividly seeing yourself performing just as you'd like to.

## 3. Exercise Regularly

One of the healthiest ways to blow off steam is to get regular exercise. Students can work exercise into their schedules by doing yoga in the morning, walking or biking to campus, or reviewing for tests with a friend while walking on a treadmill at the gym. Starting now and keeping a regular exercise practice throughout your lifetime can help you live longer and enjoy your life more.

## 4. Take Calming Breaths

When your body is experiencing a stress response, you're often not thinking as clearly as you could be. A quick way to calm down is to practice breathing exercises. These can be done virtually anywhere to relieve stress in minutes, and are especially effective for reducing anxiety before or even during tests, as well as during other times when stress feels overwhelming.

## 5. Practice Progressive Muscle Relaxation (PMR)

Another great stress reliever that can be used during tests, before bed, or at other times when stress has you physically wound up is progressive muscle relaxation (PMR). This technique involves tensing and relaxing all muscles until the body is completely relaxed.

With practice, you can learn to release stress from your body in seconds. This can be particularly helpful for students because it can be adapted to help relaxation efforts before sleep for deeper sleep, something students can always use, or even to relax and reverse test-induced panic before or during a test.

## 6. Listen to Music

A convenient stress reliever that has also shown many cognitive benefits, music can help you to relieve stress and either calm yourself down or stimulate your mind as your situation warrants. Students can harness the benefits of music by playing classical music while studying, playing upbeat music to "wake up" mentally, or relaxing with the help of their favorite slow melodies.

## 7. Get Organized

Clutter can cause stress, decrease productivity, and even cost you money. Many students live in a cluttered place, and this can have negative effects on grades. One way to reduce the amount of stress that you experience is to keep a minimalist, soothing study area that's free of distractions and clutter.

This can help lower stress levels, save time in finding lost items, and keep roommate relationships more positive. It can also help students gain a positive feeling about their study area, which helps with test prep and encourages more studying. It's worth the effort.

## 8. Eat a Healthy Diet

You may not realize it, but your diet can either boost your brainpower or sap you of mental energy. A healthy diet can function as both a stress management technique and a study aid. Improving your diet can keep you from experiencing diet-related mood swings, light-headedness, and more.

## 9. Try Self-Hypnosis

Students often find themselves "getting very sleepy" (like when they pull all-nighters), but—all kidding aside—self-hypnosis can be an effective stress management tool and a powerful productivity tool as well.

With it, you can help yourself release tension from your body and stress from your mind, and plant the seeds of success in your subconscious mind with the power of autosuggestion.

# 10. Use Positive Thinking and Affirmations

Did you know that optimists actually experience better circumstances, in part, because their way of thinking helps to *create* better circumstances in their lives? It's true! The habit of optimism and positive thinking can bring better health, baetter relationships, and, yes, better grades.

Learn how to train your brain for more positive self-talk and a brighter future with affirmations and other tools for optimism. You can also learn the limitations to affirmations and the caveats of positive thinking so you aren't working against yourself.

# Chapter 17:

# Trust The Process

Today we're going to talk about the power of having faith that things will work out for you even though you can't see the end in sight just yet. And why you need to simply trust in the process in all the things that you do.

Fear is something that we all have. We fear that if we quit our jobs to pursue our passions, that we may not be able to feed ourselves if our dreams do not work out. We fear that if we embark on a new business venture, that it might fail and we would have incurred financial and professional setbacks.

All this is borne out of the fear of the unknown. The truth is that we really do not know what can or will happen. We may try to imagine in our heads as much as we can, but we can never really know until we try and experienced it for ourselves.

The only way to overcome the fear of the unknown is to take small steps, one day at a time. We will, to the best of our ability, execute the plan that we have set for ourselves. And the rest we leave it up to the confidence that our actions will lead to results.

If problems arise, we deal with it there and then. We put out fires, we implement updated strategies, and we keep going. We keep going until we have exhausted all avenues. Until there is no more roads for us to travel, no more paths for us to create. That is the best thing that we can do.

If we constantly focus on the fear, we will never go anywhere. If we constantly worry about the future, we will never be happy with the present. If we dwell on our past failures, we will be a victim of our own shortcomings. We will not grow, we will not learn, we will not get better.

I challenge each and every one of you today to make the best out of every situation that you will face. Grab fear by the horns and toss them aside as if it were nothing. I believe in you and all that you can achieve.

Chapter 18:

# 10 Habits of Francoise Bettencourt-Meyers

Several well-known names come to mind when it comes to the wealthiest men alive. However, if you ask around about the richest woman alive, almost no one will be able to identify her. As of 2021, Francoise Meyers is the world's richest woman, owning L'Oréal, the world's largest cosmetic company.

Françoise Meyers is a French billionaire heiress with an estimated net worth of $ 93.9 billion, an author; she has written books on both Jewish and Christianity, as well as Greek mythology. She inherited L'Oréal's fortune after her mother died. Now that you know about her, what are her habits?

Here are 10 habits of Francoise Bettencourt Meyers.

### 1. She Shuns the Spotlight

Meyers, like her mother, is a very private person. According to those close to her, she is not someone you can spot from many media outlets, but you'll see her out of family controversies. Meyers is quite introverted and prefers to spend her free time playing the piano and writing despite.

### 2. She's a Serious-Minded Intellectual

Meyers has a busy career despite her lavish lifestyle. According to Tom Sancton, the L'Oreal heirless is a well-known author. She has written two books, one of which is a five-volume study of the Bible, and the other is a genealogy of Greek gods. He also noted that since Meyers is not a person you'll find making daily headlines out of nowhere, She's more confined and comfortable with her books than the outside world.

### 3. She's Less Hands-On L'Oreal Matters

You may know Liliane, her mother, as someone who could read tons of documents because L'Oreal was her lifeblood. However, that's not her daughter. Despite serving on the board for more than two decades, the billionaire heiress has shown less interest in the company than her mother. According to Sanction, she would attend meetings, but, unlike her mother, she was never hands-on.

### 4. She's charitable

Just like every other charitable billionaire you know of, Bettencourt shouldn't be exempt from your list. Meyers pledged a $226 million donation to repair the Parisian Church, according to a business insider. She is also the president of the Bettencourt Schueller Foundation, a cofounded non-profit organization that awards grants to support life science research, art projects, and other humanitarian projects.

### 5. Time Is Her Most Important Possession

Your time, according to Francoise, is the most valuable asset, and one thing for sure, once wasted, can't be recovered. So put a price tag on it, and value every inch of it. To be successful in life, you must understand the value of time.

## 6. Remains Curious

Sticking to what you know is a serious way of thinking in many corporate settings. However, according to L'Oreal heirless, you should think outside or precisely the opposite. By keeping your mind open to novel ideas and accepting curiosity, you open doors for yourself. Your scope expands by proffering yourself to a variety of intellectual resources.

## 7. She Serves Her Curiosity Very Well

According to Bettencourt, much of her life lessons came from disappointments, challenges, and losses. Although they were unpleasant, they aided her in the development of self-awareness. However, if you always wear your blinders, your perspective becomes overly narrow, and you miss out on great opportunities.

## 8. Reading Is Part of Her Daily Life

Just like Most billionaires, Francoise is a voracious reader. And according to her, reading is one of the best ways to learn new things, may reflect your curious mind. She believes that reading is essential because it will provide new ideas, challenge your current thinking, and inspire creativity.

## 9. She Had a Strained Relationship With Her Mother

Francoise's mother told Vanity Fair in 2008 that her daughter had become "something inert," which explains their rocky relationship. Even though a lawsuit was involved, it was not for Francoise's benefit but the benefit of her mother. What else can you do when you discover that your mother's lover is extorting her emotional vulnerability for a portion of your family's fortune?

## 10. She's a Family Woman

Little is known about Francoise's married life, but she was a woman until her husband's Jean-Pierre Meyers, was murdered in the Auschwitz concentration camp. Her marriage sparked controversy because of her grandfather's involvement with the Nazi government. She has two children, whom she raised according to Jewish customs.

## Conclusion

You may not be lucky enough to have been born and raised in a very wealthy family like Francoise Bettencourt, but you can, indeed, emulate one or two habits from her. Holding the title of the richest woman in the world is quite intriguing for other females with similar goals as Francoise.

## Chapter 19:

# Overcoming Tiredness and Lethargy

Tiredness and lethargy has become a major problem for youths and adults these days. As our lives get busier and our ability to control our sleep gets more out of hand, we all face a constant struggle to stay alert and engaged in our life's work every single day. And this problem hits me as well.

You see, many of us have bad sleep habits, and while it might feel good to stay up late every night to watch Netflix and binge on YouTube and Instagram posts, we pay for it the next day by being a few hours short of a restful night when our alarm wakes us up abruptly every morning.

We tell ourselves that not needing so much sleep is fine for us, but our body tells us a different story. And we can only fake being energetic and awake for so long. Sooner or later we will no doubt experience the inability to function on an optimal level and our productivity and mood will also be affected accordingly. And this would also lead to overall tiredness and lethargy in the long run.

Before we talk about what we can do to counter and fix this problem that we have created for ourselves, we first have to understand why we consciously allow ourselves to become this tired in the first place.

I believe that many of us choose entertainment over sleep every night is because we are in some ways or another overworked to the point that we don't have enough time to ourselves every single day that we choose to sacrifice our sleep time in order to gain back that few hours of quality personal time. After spending a good 10 hours at our jobs from 9-6pm, and after settling down from the commute home and factoring in dinner time, we find ourselves with only a solid 1-2 hours of time to watch our favourite Netflix shows or YouTube, which i believe is not very much time for the average person.

When presented with the choice of sleep versus another episode or two of our guilty pleasure, it becomes painfully obvious which is the "better" choice for us. And we either knowingly or unknowingly choose entertainment and distraction over health.

Basically, I believe the amount of sleep you choose to give yourself is directly proportionate to how happy you are about your job. Because if you can't wait to get up each and everyday to begin your life's work, you will give yourself the best possible sleep you can each night to make sure you are all fired up the next day to crush your work. But conversely, if you hate your job and you feel like you have wasted all your time at work all day, you will ultimately feel that you will need to claim that time back at night to keep yourself sane and to keep yourself in the job no matter how much you dislike it. Even if it means sacrificing precious sleep to get there.

So I believe the real question is not how can we force ourselves to sleep earlier every night to get the 8 hours of sleep that we need in order not to feel tired and lethargic, but rather is there anything we can change about how we view our job and work that we come home at the end of the day feeling recharged and fulfilled to the extend that we don't have to look for a way to escape every night into the world of entertainment just to fill our hearts.

When you have found something you love to do each day, you will have no trouble going to bed at 10pm each night instead of 1 or 2am.

So I challenge each and everyone of you to take a hard look at WHY you are not getting enough sleep. There is a high chance that it could boil down to the reason I have described here today, and maybe a change in careers might be something to consider. But if you believe that this tiredness and lethargy is born out of something medical and genetic, then please do go see a doctor to get a medical solution to it.

**Chapter 20:**

# _Happy People Stay Grateful For Everything They Have_

A lot of us will have different answers to this simple question, "what are you grateful for today?" It could differ from as simple as getting out of bed to achieving that huge task you had your mind on for a while. Gratitude is the emotion we feel when we tend to notice and appreciate the good things that have come into our lives. Some people feel grateful for even the tiniest things, while others don't even if they achieve more than they have wished for. Most of the time, people who will be thankful still feel negative emotions, but they tend to shift their focus from all the bad things in their lives to the good ones.

Research has shown that teenagers and adults who feel more grateful than others are also happier, get better grades, have better friends, get more opportunities, have fewer illnesses and pain, have more energy, and tend to sleep better. The link of practicing gratitude to achieve happiness is through a path that we commonly call the "cognitive pathway." The words "cognitive" and "cognition" are used by scientists to talk about thinking; if we don't think about the good things in our life, we would not feel grateful.

Most situations that happen in our lives are neither all good nor all bad. It is on us how we trick our minds and interpret the effect of the situation on our lives. One of the thinking habits is called a "positive interpretation bias," which means that we are most likely to interpret a neutral or negative situation positively. On the contrary, some people tend to ignore all the positive aspects of their problems and finds excuses and reasons to focus more on the negativity.

Studies also show that people who practice gratitude remember more good memories than bad ones. A more grateful person tends to encode more positive memories and keeps out the negative ones. They are also tended to be healthier and are sick less often. This is because they worry less about all the wrong things and focus more on the positive stuff they had achieved throughout the days. They keep their negative emotions to a minimum. A study showed that people who felt more grateful also had increased brain activity essential for both emotional and cognitive processes.

Happiness and gratitude go hand in hand and can be practiced in a lot of different ways. One way is to write a list of all the good things that have happened to you every day and go through it before you sleep. Another way is to send some love to your close ones, thanking and appreciating all that they have done for you. While it is essential to practice gratitude every day, it is also important to know that the bad things shouldn't be ignored. In fact, the real test of gratitude is how we act on the situations when they don't go as per our plans. We don't always need to be happy to be grateful, but gratitude indeed leads to greater happiness.

# Chapter 21:

# The Magic of the 5 Minute Rule

Recently I have been struggling to get things done, more so than usual. It has become a daily battle with myself to sit down on my desk to begin the necessary work that I know i need to do. However looking at the endless list of tasks i have in front of me, i can't help but to choose procrastination and slacking over beginning my work. And it has affected my ability to be a productive member of society.

Whilst I knew in the back of my mind that I believe the work that I do can benefit society, and that it has the power to give me freedom of time and money to get and do the things that i really wanted to do in life, on some level it wasn't actually enough to get me to start the work. Many a times I felt really sluggish and it would take some strong reminders to get me motivated enough to start the work. That was the point where i decided i needed to search for a solution that work not only make work more enjoyable, but to also push me to get work started much faster without delay.

After spending some solid hours researching, i came across one strategy that I felt would work like a charm on me. And that is to employ the 5 minute rule to every single task that I have on hand.

The biggest problem that I have currently is that I am working on 10 different projects at any one time. And when I look at these 10 separate projects that need my attention, I can't help but feel overwhelmed about the number of hours that I needed to schedule for each of these projects. And that seemed like a mountainous task for me to climb. And looking at it as a whole, it felt absolutely daunting and impossible. Which was what made me not want to even attempt to begin that climb.

How the 5 minute rule works is that for every project that I needed to work on, I wrote that I only needed to do the task for 5 minutes. However ridiculous that sounded, it actually worked like a charm. My brain was tricked into thinking that this became much more manageable and i would accomplish it easily. And we all know that the biggest problem is getting started. But once u do, you tend to keep going. And so for every task that i told myself i needed to do for 5 minutes, in reality i ended up spending the adequate amount of time i needed to do to get the job done. whether it be 10 minutes, 30minutes, an hour, or even several hours.

I managed to trick my brain into breaking each project down to its most basic manageable form and that gave me to confidence that I could crush it with ease. I applied this technique to not only work, but also going to the gym, walking my dog, and other administrative and personal tasks that I was lazy to do. And i saw my ability to begin each task and eventually check it off my to-do list increase exponentially. My productivity level also skyrocketed as a result.

With this simple trick in your arsenal. I believe anyone that you too can begin your work much quicker as well and crush every single task that will be put in front of you today and in your future. So i challenge each and every one of you today to just tell yourself that you will only need to set aside 5 mins for each task and see where that takes you, and that I believe will be in the right direction.

# Chapter 22:

# 10 Habits That Can Ruin Your Day

Habits are the building blocks of our day. No matter how you spin it, either way, every detail matters.

The little actionable habits eventually sets you up to a either having a fulfilling day, or one that you have just totally wasted away. Nothing is as bad as destructive habits as they sabotage your daily productivity. Slowly, you slip further and further until it's too late when you've realized the damage that they have done to your life.

Bad habits are insidious! They drag down your life, lowers down your levels of accuracy, and make your performance less creative and stifling. It is essential, not only for productivity, to gain control of your bad habits. AS Grenville Kleiser once noted, "Constant self-discipline and self-control help you develop greatness of character." Nonetheless, it is important to stop and ask: what do you need today to get rid of or change? Sure, you can add or adjust new skills into your daily life.

Below are ten persistent habits that can ruin your day's success and productivity.

## 1. Hitting The Snooze Button.

Your mind, while you sleep, moves through a comprehensive series of cycles, the last one alerting you to wake up. While you crave for ten more minutes of sleep as the alarm goes off, what do you do? You whacked the snooze button. We're all guilty of this! If you don't suck it up, rip off the cover and start your morning, the rest of your day will be flawed.

How do you expect your day to be strong once you don't start it off strong? You will feel far more optimistic, strong and fully prepared when you wake up without hitting the snooze button. So avoid the snooze button at any cost if you want a productive day ahead!

## 2. Wasting Your "Getting Ready" Hours.

You might need to reconsider the scrolling of Instagram and Facebook or the inane program you put on behind the scenes while preparing. These things have a time and place to partake in them – for example when you've accomplished your day's work and need some time to unwind and relax; however the time isn't now. Your morning schedule ought to be an interaction that prepares and energizes you for the day ahead. The objective is to accomplish something that animates your mind within the first hour of being conscious, so you can be more inventive, invigorated, gainful, and connected with all through the entire day! Avoiding this sweeps you away from normalizing the worst habit you might have: distraction. Instead, give yourself a chance to breathe the fine morning, anticipate the day's wonder and be thankful for whatever you have.

## 3. Failing To Prioritize Your Breakfast.

Energizing your day is essential if you wish for a very productive day. Energizing your body system requires that you prioritize eating your breakfast. However, the contents of your breakfast must entail something that will ensure that your day is not slowed down by noon. This means a blend of high - fiber foods such as proteins and healthy must be incorporated. Avoid taking too many sugars and heavy starches. The goal is to satiate and energize your body for the day.

## 4. Ruminating on the Problems of Yesterday And Negativity.

Don't take yesterday's problems to your new day if you want to start your day off right. If the day before you had difficult meetings and talks and you woke up ruminating about your horrific experiences, leave that negativity at your doorway. Moreover, if the problem you are lamenting about have been solved, then you shouldn't dwell on the past. Research suggests that we usually encounter more positive than negative events in a day. Still, often your mind concentrates on the negative due to a subconscious distortion called the negative distortion. By choosing not to focus on negative events and thinking about what's going well, you can learn to take advantage of the strength of the positive events around us. Raising negativity only increases stress. Let go of it and get on without it!

## 5. Leaving Your Day To Randomness.

Do not let stuff just simply happen to you; do it. Failure to create a structured day leads to a totally random day. A random day lacking direction, focus, and efficiency. Distractions will also creep into your day more readily because you have allowed randomness to happen to you. Instead, have a clear and precise list of what you need to focus for the day. This serves as a framework and a boundary for you to work within. Another thing you should consider is to spend your first 90 minutes on the most thoughtful and important task for the day. This allows you to know the big things out right at the beginning, reducing your cognitive burden for the rest of the day.

## 6. Becoming Involved With the Overview.

How frequently have you woken up, and before you can stretch and grin, you groan pretty much all the have-to for now and the fragmented musts from yesterday? This unhealthy habit will ruin your great day ahead. Know and understand these are simply contemplations. You can decide to recalibrate by pondering all you must be thankful for and searching for the splendid focuses in your day. Shift thinking, and you'll begin the day empowered.

## 7. Overscheduling and Over-Engagement.

People tend to underestimate how long things take with so many things to do. This habit of overscheduling and over-engagement can quickly lead to burn out. Always ensure that you permit extra time and energy for the unforeseen. Take regular breaks and don't overcommit to other people. This gives you more freedom for yourself and you won't be running the risk of letting others down by not turning up. Try not to overestimate what you can complete, so you won't feel like a disappointment. Be sensible and practical with your scheduling. Unexpectedly and eventually, you'll complete more.

## 8. Postponing or Discarding the Tough Tasks.

We have a restricted measure of mental energy, and as we exhaust this energy, our dynamic and efficiency decrease quickly. This is called decision exhaustion. Running the bad habit of postponing and disregarding the tough tasks will trigger this reaction in us. At the point when you put off extreme assignments till late in the day because they're scary, you deplete more and more of your mental resources. To beat choice weariness, you should handle complex assignments toward the beginning of the day when your brain is new.

## 9. Failure To Prioritize Your Self-Care.

Work, family commitments, and generally talking of the general obligations give almost everyone an awesome excuse to let your self-care rehearses pass by the wayside. Achievement-oriented minds of individuals see how basic self-care is to their expert achievement. Invest energy doing things that bring you delight and backing your psychological and actual wellbeing. "Success" doesn't exclusively apply to your finances or expert accomplishments.

# 10. Waiting for the Easier Way Out / Waiting for the Perfect Hack of Your Life.

The most noticeably awful everyday habit is trusting that things will occur and for a chance to thump at your entryway. As such, you become an inactive onlooker, not a proactive part of your own life. Once in a while, it shows itself as the quest for simple little-known techniques. Rather than getting down to work, ineffective individuals search how to take care of job quicker for quite a long time. Try not to begin with a #lifehack search on the internet unless it really does improve your productivity without sacrificing the necessary steps you need to take each day to achieve holistic success.

## ✓ Merging It All Together

A portion of these habits may appear to be minor, yet they add up. Most amount to an individual decision between immediate pleasures and enduring ones. The most exceedingly awful propensity is forgetting about what matters to you. Always remember that you are just one habit away from changing you life forever.

## Chapter 23:

# How To Fall In Love With Boredom And Unlock Your Mental Toughness

First, there is very little hope for falling in love with a habit that you truly hate. I don't know anyone who legitimately dislikes an activity and somehow falls in love with doing it. It doesn't add up. It's very difficult to hate something and be in love with it at the same time. (Your ex doesn't count.)

Let's say you dislike working out, but you know it's good for you. If you want to <u>fall in love with the boredom of going to the gym</u>, then you have two options.

## OPTION 1: INCREASE YOUR PROFICIENCY AT THE TASK

Even tasks that you are good at will feel monotonous some days, so imagine the uphill battle you're fighting if you are constantly trying to do something that you don't feel skilled at. The solution? Learn the fundamentals of your task and celebrate the small wins and improvements you make. With our workout example, let's say you purchase <u>Starting Strength</u> and learn how to do a proper deadlift or bench press. Practicing these new skills in the gym can be fun, and making tiny improvements each week builds momentum. It's much easier to fall in love with doing something over and over again if you can look forward to making progress.

## OPTION 2: FALL IN LOVE WITH THE RESULT OF THE TASK RATHER THAN THE TASK ITSELF

Let's be real: there are some things that we should do that are always going to be a hassle. Running sprints might be an example. Very few people look forward to setting their lungs on fire.

I have more success in situations like these when I shift my focus away from the actual task and toward a result. Sometimes this is a direct result of the habit I'm trying to perform. Other times, it's a result that I invent. For example, you can make a game out of not missing workouts even if you don't enjoy the workout itself. Let's say you have done two sprint workouts in a row. Your goal is to fall in love with becoming the type of person who doesn't miss workouts. You're not worried about how you perform. You're not worried about if you're getting faster. You're not worried about getting six-pack abs or any other type of result. For the most part, you're not even thinking about the workout. Instead, you're simply focused on keeping your workout streak alive.

This is the Seinfeld Strategy applied to exercise. Your only goal is to "not break the chain." By shifting your focus away from the activity you dislike, you're allowing yourself to fall in love with the boredom of sticking to the streak (something you do enjoy).

# Chapter 24:

# 7 Ways To Stop Overthinking And Relieve Stress

The way you respond to your thoughts can sometimes keep you in a cycle of <u>rumination</u>, or repetitive thinking. The next time you find yourself continuously running things over in your mind, take note of how it affects your mood. Do you feel irritated, nervous, or guilty? What's the primary emotion behind your thoughts? Having self-awareness is key to changing your mindset.

## 1. Find a distraction

Shut down overthinking by involving yourself in an activity you enjoy. This looks different for everyone, but ideas include:

- learning some new kitchen skills by tackling a new recipe
- going to your favorite workout class
- taking up a new hobby, such as painting
- volunteering with a local organization

## 2. Take a deep breath

You've heard it a million times, but that's because it works. The next time you find yourself tossing and turning over your thoughts, close your eyes and <u>breathe deeply</u>.

Try it

Here's a good starter exercise to help you unwind with your breath:

- Find a comfortable place to sit and relax your neck and shoulders.
- Place one hand over your heart and the other across your belly.
- Inhale and exhale through your nose, paying attention to how your chest and stomach move as you breathe.

Try doing this exercise three times a day for 5 minutes, or whenever you have racing thoughts.

## 3. Meditate

Developing a regular meditation practice is an <u>evidence-backed</u> way to help clear your mind of nervous chatter by turning your attention inward.

Look at the bigger picture

How will all the issues floating around in your mind affect you 5 or 10 years from now? Will anyone really care that you bought a fruit plate for the potluck instead of baking a pie from scratch?

Don't let minor issues turn into significant hurdles.

Do something nice for someone else

Trying to ease the load for someone else can help you put things in perspective. Think of ways you can be of service to someone going through a difficult time.

Does your friend who's in the middle of a divorce need a few hours of childcare? Can you pick up groceries for your neighbor who's been sick?

Realizing you have the power to make someone's day better can keep negative thoughts from taking over. It also gives you something productive to focus on instead of your never-ending stream of thoughts.

## 4. Recognize automatic negative thinking

Automated negative thoughts (ANTs) refer to knee-jerk negative thoughts, usually involving fear or anger, you sometimes have in reaction to a situation.

Tackling ANTs

You can identify and work through your ANTs by keeping a record of your thoughts and actively working to change them:

Use a notebook to track the situation giving you anxiety, your mood, and the first thought that comes to you automatically.

As you dig into details, evaluate why the situation is causing these negative thoughts.

Break down the emotions you're experiencing and try to identify what you're telling yourself about the situation.

Find an alternative to your original thought. For example, instead of jumping straight to, "This is going to be an epic failure," try something along the lines of, "I'm genuinely trying my best.

## 5. Acknowledge your successes

When you're in the midst of overthinking, stop and take out your notebook or your favorite note-taking app on your phone. Jot down five things that have gone right over the past week and your role in them.

These don't need to be huge accomplishments. Maybe you stuck to your coffee budget this week or cleaned out your car. When you look at it on paper or on-screen, you might be surprised at how these little things add up.

If it feels helpful, refer back to this list when you find your thoughts spiralling.

## 6. Stay present

Not ready to commit to a meditation routine? There are plenty of other ways to ground yourself in the present moment.

Be here now

Here are a few ideas:

Unplug. Shut off your computer or phone for a designated amount of time each day, and spend that time on a single activity.

Eat mindfully. Treat yourself to one of your favorite meals. Try to find the joy in each bite, and really focus on how the food tastes, smells, and feels in your mouth.

Get outside. Take a walk outside, even if it's just a quick lap around the block. Take inventory of what you see along the way, noting any smells that waft by or sounds you hear.

## 7. Consider other viewpoints

Sometimes, quieting your thoughts requires stepping outside of your usual perspective. How you see the world is shaped by your life experiences, values, and assumptions. Imagining things from a different point of view can help you work through some of the noise

## Chapter 25:

# Happy People Are Proactive About Relationships

Researchers have found that as human beings we are only capable of maintaining up to 150 meaningful relationships, including five primary, close relationships.

This holds true even with the illusion of thousands of "friends" on social media platforms such as Facebook, Instagram, and Twitter. If you think carefully about your real interactions with people, you'll find the five close/150 extended relationships rule holds true.

Perhaps not coincidentally, Tony Robbins, the personal development expert, and others argue that your attitudes, behavior, and success in life are the sum total of your five closest relationships. So, toxic relationships, toxic life.

With this in mind, it's essential to continue to develop relationships that are positive and beneficial. **But in today's distracted world, these relationships won't just happen.**

**We need to be proactive about developing our relationships.**

My current favorite book on personal development is Tim Ferriss's excellent, though long, 700+ page book, *Tools of Titans: The Tactics, Routines, and Habits of Billionaires, Icons, and World-Class Performers.*

At one point, Ferriss quotes retired women's volleyball great Gabby Reece:

*I always say that I'll go first.... That means if I'm checking out at the store, I'll say "hello" first. If I'm coming across somebody and make eye contact, I'll smile first. [I wish] people would experiment with that in their life a little bit: be first, because — not all times, but most times — it comes in your favor... The response is pretty amazing.... I was at the park the other day with the kids.*

*Oh, my God. Hurricane Harbor [water park]. It's like hell. There were these two women a little bit older than me. We couldn't be more different, right? And I walked by them, and I just looked at them and smiled. The smile came to their face so instantly. They're ready, but you have to go first because now we're being trained in this world [to opt out] — nobody's going first anymore.*

## Be proactive: start the conversation

I agree. I was excited to read this principle because I adopted this by default years ago, and it's given me the opportunity to hear the most amazing stories and develop the greatest relationships you can imagine.

On airplanes, in the grocery store, at lunch, I've started conversations that led to trading heartfelt stories, becoming friends, or doing business together. A relationship has to start someplace, and that can be any place in any moment.

## Be proactive: lose your fear of being rejected

I also love this idea because it will help overcome one of the main issues I hear from my training and coaching clients – the fear of making an initial connection with someone they don't know.

**This fear runs deep for many people and may be hardwired in humans.** We are always observing strangers to determine if we can trust them – whether they have positive or dangerous intent.

In addition, **we fear rejection. Our usual negative self-talk says something like,** *If I start the conversation, if I make eye contact, if I smile, what if it's not returned?*

*What if I'm rejected, embarrassed, or ignored by no response? I'll feel like an idiot, a needy loser.*

## Chapter 26:

# _Resist Temptations For Success_

We all have hopes and dreams. We have a rough sketch of what we want to become and what we want to achieve. Most of us have good intentions for those things too.

But the reality is that process of achieving those things isn't always as simple as we all anticipate. It is all mixed up with all these temptations that are equally alluring and want us to give up everything else for just a moment and enjoy what we are about to indulge in.

You see if you were to make a milestone for a week where you were to lose a pound of weight with rigorous cardio and hours of strict training followed by a strict diet plan. You can't say you won't be tempted by the smell of fries and fried chicken whenever you walk past one.

Surely you would be OK, only if you resisted it and kept walking your way. But if you were to pick up one piece and put it in your mouth, you just destroyed the whole mantra of self-control and self-discipline.

Self-discipline is not just putting your life on track and following a timetable. Self-discipline is not punishing yourself for any mistake. Self-discipline is following a course of actions that will take you to your ultimate goal.

We all are susceptible to weaknesses. We often end up acting against the things and goals that we value the most.

Temptations are nature's way of testing us. It is a test to evaluate our core values and our integrity. It is a litmus test to pick the leaders out of a faction. Temptations are a way of self-analyzing ourselves whether we are worthy enough or are we still distracted with all the shiny things lying around.

It is easy to get a good grade with a little help from here and there. It is easy to follow someone else's path rather than carving our own. It is easier to fake some lab results to be enrolled into a team of representatives.

But when we get the chance to do those things in real life without any outside help on an open stage where the world is judging us, we cannot get ourselves to do any of those things because we cheated n the first place and never engaged the creative factory of our mind.

So how should you approach this problem? It is a simple step-by-step process.

Start by removing the temptations. Check for any loopholes in your environment and kick them out to keep them away long enough till you are more in control.

Next, you need to take some time to think about your way of thinking as an unbiased and nonhuman object. Try to find the flaws and reinvent them to disengage any magnets in your personality that keep attracting you to those temptations.

Last but not the least, put a zipper on your pocket and control your spending habits and you will get away from any unnecessary temptation leading you to a better successful life!

# Chapter 27:

## _Improve Everything By 1%_

There is a concept in the athletic world known as the "Aggregation of Marginal Gains." It was first presented by Dave Brailsford, a performance coach for the British Cycling team.

He used to explain it as the "The 1% percent margin for improvement is always present for anything we do." What this means is that if you improve everything associated with your game by just 1 percent, these small changes will add up to show up as remarkable and rapid improvements.

We live a life of constant pushing and pulling, where we don't know what is going on and why is it happening but we still keep up with it because it is a job and not an option. But the truth is that we are not going anywhere anytime soon because we have not aced the art of living by perfection yet.

We cannot be perfect no matter what we try or what we get, but we can improve and it might get us better than most.

So how does this rule work? It is simple!

You take one aspect of your life and you work towards making a single thing better at a time. Let's say you were to start a business and have had your fair share of failures for all these years. So what to do now for a changed outcome?

You could start off by choosing a better thing to sell. You can look for better producers for better buying prices. The next thing you can do is to find better means of selling over the traditional mediums. And if you are e done that already, you can look for better markets to sell.

The right approach for a process lies in the small details that lead you to the final model.

There is always room for improvement in every aspect of life and this is the philosophy that we all lack. We expect things to get better once and for all in a single instant. But improvement is a time taking process and a constantly changing process.

We have convinced ourselves that change is only a meaningful thing once we have a large and prominent outcome that comes along. We expect to get bigger and better gains over an unrealistic amount of time with absolutely none to minimal effort.

I am not saying that you need to leave everything else and devote all your energies and time to a single target. But you need to improve little by little with small changes that are prominent on their own level. The results will improve but that will take some time and all you can do is hope for the best.

Improvement by 1% isn't noticeable for even the most alert people, but not trying it is the biggest blunder anyone can do. Your success is like your life cycle. You wait for getting taller, you wait for growing adult features and you wait for getting your first paycheck. Why do you expect to see results in one go?

# Chapter 28: *How To Have Proper Time Management*

Managing time is one of the hardest things to do; our everyday routine revolves around time management. But what does it mean? Some people fail to understand the true meaning of time management. Time management can be defined as planning and controlling how much time to spend on specific activities. When a person knows how to manage his time, he faces less stress and efficiently completes more work in less time.

Everyone now wants to manage their time, the world is moving fast, so must we, but how to do that? The answer is relatively easy. You need to set your goals correctly. Setting your goals correctly would help you save time and so your brain wouldn't be messed up. The SMART method is the best method, where s stands for specific, M stands for measurable, A stands for attainable, R stands for relevant, and T stands for timely. If you set your goals by using the SMART method, you are bound to manage your time.

Now sometimes we all have so much work to do that we forget which one is more important, what you should do is to sit back for a minute, take out your to-do list and see which of your daily task is both important as well as urgent than that task should be your priority and you should do these tasks right away. Some tasks are important but not urgent, you can decide when to do these, but some are neither critical nor urgent you can leave them later to do. Prioritizing your tasks properly helps you manage time.

We all say that this generation is moving fast, but we also know that laziness is in the air. Being lazy is what messes up our routine. "Time is money" we all have heard this but hardly pay attention to this; wasting our time on one task is like ruining our whole plan for the day. You need to set a time limit for every task, depending on its difficulty level. When you have been assigned something to do, estimate the time it would take you to complete that task and set a limit. If you think you don't have enough time to complete the task, then seeking help from someone is not a bad option. But if you don't check the time, you may end up with incomplete work that will cause you a few problems.

Although work is essential, "All work and no play makes Jack a dull boy," this means that when a person is constantly working and burdens himself with the workload, he finds it hard to concentrate because his brain is all fried up. When you have a busy and packed schedule that includes many tasks, try to take small breaks between these tasks. Working constantly will make it hard for you to focus on your next task. You should take a break in the middle of these tasks, try grabbing a brief nap, or you can do something that will freshen up your brain like meditation, jogging, etc.

An organized person feels less messed up; for example, even if your wardrobe is messed up, you feel uncomfortable because this nagging sensation at the back of your head tells you that your closet needs to be organized. Similarly, try managing your calendar for more long-term time management. Try writing on a calendar about appointments, meetings, deadlines, so you don't forget what to do next. If there is something you need to do, then set a few days for that specific task. This method will help you remember more of your task and your plans.

Although time management is hard, it is not impossible. You just need to prioritise, take small breaks and sort out everything and you would be good to go.

# Chapter 29:

# HOW TO STOP JUDGING YOUR OWN WORK

Have you been extra nice to yourself lately? If you're a writer ... the answer is probably: "...mayyyybe?"

Writers — creators in general — are way too hard on themselves. We like making things, and we feel good doing it. But we really want to feel like we're doing a good job.

When we don't feel that way — which happens much more often than we realize — we start to doubt if writing is even worth the struggle.

Why are we so judgmental of our own work? Because it's the easiest to judge. It comes from us. We know it better than anyone.

But we can all learn to be critical without being so harsh. Here's how.

**Remind yourself that not everything you write is going to feel polished.** And the simple reason for that? The majority of the time, it won't be.

You have to make messes to make masterpieces. You have to do things wrong, you have to not do your best if you're ever going to learn what you're actually capable of. If what you're writing seems terrible — well, it might be. That doesn't mean it always will be, or that it will be the best thing you'll ever write.

You're going to write sentences you're unsure of, paragraphs that just don't "sound quite right." You're going to question whether or not this scene should stay or go. You're going to ask yourself a million times if you're doing any of this right.

What matters most is that you keep writing anyway. You can't polish something unfinished. Even if a draft feels like the worst thing you've ever written, at least you have something to work with — something you can improve little by little until it meets your personal standards (if that's even possible ...).

**Focus on how you feel about your work, not on how others might react.** We're all guilty of imagining how our future readers will react to certain parts of our stories. Sometimes, it's what keeps you going when you're starting to feel unsure. When you laugh at your own writing (admit it — it happens to you too), you picture others laughing too.

But there's a dark side to this train of thought. If we focus too much on what people might think about our writing, we can begin to worry that they won't like it. That they'll tell everyone else not to read it. That our words aren't actually good ... that they never will be.

The best way to judge whether or not your writing is meaningful and readable is if it feels that way to you. Yes, your readers matter whether they exist yet or not. You are writing for their entertainment. But until you get your words in front of eyes, the only opinion that matters is yours.

**Your inner critic will never stop talking, but you can tune it out.** Here's the truth not every writing expert will tell you: you will never stop doubting or judging yourself or your writing. There is no magic cure for self-criticism. But that doesn't mean you can't tone it down enough to avoid letting it interfere with your work.

We judge ourselves more harshly than everyone else does (even though it sometimes feels the other way around) because we genuinely want to do a good job. And deep down we know we are the only ones in control of whether or not we do the work "well."

The problem is, we're so used to seeing others' work and the kinds of writing that gets high praise that we often can't help but compare our drafts to their published masterpieces. When we do that, our writing just never feels "as good." We immediately spiral into "i'll never be good enough" self-talk. We get sad. We stop writing.

That negative self-talk will always be there. You will always hear it.

But you don't have to listen to it.

You don't have to care about the lies it's telling you. You don't have to let them stop you from doing the work you know you're meant to do.

It's one thing to say you're not going to pay attention to your voice of doubt and another to actually ignore it. It's not that simple for a lot of people — and that's ok. Some have an easier time quieting their minds than others. As a writer, it's often one of those things you learn to do the longer you do it, the more you practice it.

That voice in your head telling you that you'll never achieve your dreams?

The best thing you can do to demote its scream to a whisper is to prove it wrong.

## Chapter 30:

# 8 Steps To Develop Beliefs That Will Drive you To Success

'Success' is a broad term. There is no universal definition of success, it varies from person to person considering their overall circumstances. We can all more or less agree that confidence plays a key role in it, and confidence comes from belief.

Even our most minute decisions and choices in life are a result of believing in some specific outcome that we have not observed yet.

However, merely believing in an ultimate success will not bring fortune knocking at your door. But, it certainly can get you started—take tiny steps that might lead you towards your goal. Now, since we agree that having faith can move you towards success, let's look at some ways to rewire your brain into adopting productive beliefs.

Here are 8 Steps to Develop Beliefs That Will Drive You To Success:

### 1. Come Up With A Goal

Before you start, you need to decide what you want to achieve first. Keep in mind that you don't have to come up with something very specific right away because your expectations and decisions might change over time. Just outline a crude sense of what 'Achievement' and 'Success' mean to you in the present moment.

Begin here. Begin now. Work towards getting there.

## 2. Put Your Imagination Into Top Gear

"Logic will take you from A to B. Imagination will take you everywhere", said Albert Einstein.

Imagination is really important in any scenario whatsoever. It is what makes us humans different from animals. It is what gives us a reason to move forward—it gives us hope. And from that hope, we develop the will to do things we have never done before.

After going through the first step of determining your goal, you must now imagine yourself being successful in the near future. You have to literally picture yourself in the future, enjoying your essence of fulfilment as vividly as you can. This way, your ultimate success will appear a lot closer and realistic.

## 3. Write Notes To Yourself

Writing down your thoughts on paper is an effective way to get those thoughts stuck in your head for a long time. This is why children are encouraged to write down what is written in the books instead of memorizing them just by reading. You have to write short, simple, motivating notes to yourself that will encourage you to take actions towards your success. It doesn't matter whether you write in a notebook, or on your phone or wherever—just write it. On top of that, occasionally read what you've written and thus, you will remain charged with motivation at all times.

## 4. Make Reading A Habit

There are countless books written by successful people just so that they can share the struggle and experience behind their greatest achievements. In such an abundance of manuscripts, you may easily find books that portray narratives similar to your life and circumstances. Get reading and expand your knowledge. You'll get never-thought-before ideas that will guide you through your path to success. Reading such books will tremendously strengthen your faith in yourself, and in your success. Read what other successful people believed in—what drove them. You might even find newer beliefs to hold on to. No wonder why books are called 'Man's best friend'.

## 5. Talk To People Who Motivates You

Before taking this step, you have to be very careful about who you talk to. Basically, you have to speak out your goals and ambitions in life to someone who will be extremely supportive of you. Just talk to them about what you want, share your beliefs and they will motivate you from time to time towards success. They will act as powerful reminders. Being social beings, no human can ever reject the gist of motivation coming from another human being—especially when that is someone whom you can rely on comfortably. Humans have been the sole supporter of each other since eternity.

## 6. Make A Mantra

Self-affirming one-liners like 'I can do it', 'Nothing can stop me', 'Success is mine' etc. will establish a sense of firm confidence in your subconscious mind. Experts have been speculative about the power of our subconscious mind for long. The extent of what it can do is still beyond our grasp. But nonetheless, reciting subtle mantras isn't a difficult task. Do it a couple of times every day and it will remain in your mind for ages, without you giving any conscious thought to it. Such subconscious affirmations may light you up in the right moment and show you the path to success when you least expect it.

## 7. Reward Yourself From Time To Time

Sometimes, your goals might be too far-fetched and as a result, you'll find it harder to believe in something so improbable right now. In a situation like this, what you can do is make short term objectives that ultimately lead to your main goal and for each of those objectives achieved, treat yourself with a reward of any sort—absolutely anything that pleases you. This way, your far cry success will become more apparent to you in the present time. Instant rewards like these will also keep you motivated and make you long for more. This will drive you to believe that you are getting there, you are getting closer and closer to success.

8.   Having Faith In Yourself

Your faith is in your hands alone. How strongly you believe in what you deserve will motivate you. It will steer the way for self-confidence to fulfill your inner self. You may be extremely good at something but due to the lack of faith in your own capabilities, you never attempted it—how will you ever know that you were good at that? Your faith in yourself and your destined success will materialize before you through these rewards that you reserve for yourself. You absolutely deserve this!

Final Thoughts

That self-confidence and belief and yourself, in your capabilities and strengths will make you work towards your goal. Keep in mind that whatever you believe in is what you live for. At the end of the day, each of us believed in something that made us thrive, made us work and move forward. Some believed in the military, some believed in maths, some believed in thievery—everyone had a belief which gave them a purpose—the purpose of materializing their belief in this world. How strongly you hold onto your belief will decide how successful you will become.

## Chapter 31:

# 10 Habits of Mukesh Ambani

From managing his father-founded company to becoming India's most affluent and business tycoon, Mukesh Ambani knows, thinks, and does certain things which you don't. Mukesh chairs and runs multi-billion Reliance Industries, which accounts for a hefty 5percent of India's GDP. Without a doubt, he's indeed leading a very successful and wealthy life.

If you were to ask Mukesh Ambani about his rise to success, he would have to speak from years of experience. But, because he's a guru, not just a "talker," he believes that whatever comes of you is a direct result of your understanding of the nature of your business. So, what is his path to success?

Here are 10 habits of Mukesh Ambani.

## 1. Speak Less, Do More

Israel More's quote "talk less, do more" perfectly describes Mukesh's approach to progress. He not only keeps small social circles, but he also avoids scandals as much as possible. He's the type of person who will advise you to stand your ground by focusing on your business and possibly avoid politicking. Despite being India's most talked-about business personality, he does not promote or stimulate the attention he receives.

## 2. Treat the Investor's Money With Caution

Ambani believes that you should treat your investors' money with more care than your own. It's a chicken and egg situation, but it appears to go hand in hand with high investor confidence. It is unknown whether his success came before his special handling of investors' money. Still, he is the polar opposite of how many businesses treat the investment as if they have hit the lottery.

## 3. Money Is the By-Product of Success

Most successful people, including Musk and Jack Ma, have talked against holding money-driven motivation when carrying on your business. Accordingly, Mukesh's father also believed that chasing money won't guarantee success. He founded Reliance with the same thought, which Mukesh carried on after taking over, and he's now reaping the benefits.

## 4. Dream Big

Dreaming big goes hand in hand with working hard to make it a reality. Words may ring dull, but how can a business materialize without a vision and a plan to guide it? As Mukesh stated during his "Global Living Legends" acceptance speech, "align your passion with your life goal and pursue the goal with excellence, and success will chase you."

## 5. Nurture Your Staff, Not the Profits

Ambani has primarily built his company by taking the bold step of assembling the right team. He believes in an organizational culture that demonstrates empathy, fosters trust and relationships, and views mistakes as learning opportunities. To bring out the best in your employees, create a work environment that nurtures their skills and talents. And you can only do this if you prioritize employees over profits.

## 6. Credibility Conveys a High Premium

Ambani advises on being there whenever it is your team that needs you or the competition. Recognize, innovate, and plan for the future. He believes that, in addition to cash inflow and outflow, credibility must be protected.

## 7. Risks Give the Most Vital Insights

Sometime back in 2015, Ambani made a risky decision, which many thought was too risky. That is, his decision to roll out 4G; yes, you read that correctly! 4G is a mobile phone network. He once said that if you do not take risks, you will not experience significant growth in your life. And, yes, he proved this throughout his career.

## 8. See Everyone as a Potential Customer

According to Ambani's target market strategy, a billion people means a billion potential customers. There is no way he will let customers slip through his reach, thus taking the chance to generate value for them and, in return, making something for himself. When you consider how populated India is, you can see the volumes business people in this part of the world have to sell.

## 9. Trust All, but Rely on No One

Ambani believes in being your drive to succeed. Yes, you will need to be around people, but you need not rely on anyone but yourself for business success. While he has a trusted team of a few people who have played critical roles in expanding his empire, Ambani understands that nothing beats perseverance and self-learning. Trust is important, but you must keep abreast of all types of emergencies that keep the company running.

## 10. Trust Your Gut Instincts

There have been several controversies concerning Mukesh, 'a rich man without a heart' owing to his splurging money on building his house and investing in the IPL cricket team. However, Mukesh does what he deems suitable, and most of it turns out to be "right thing to do" for him. Follow your instincts and disregard anyone's opinion especially when it doesn't add value to you, and because haters are always a mile away.

## Conclusion

What more! He is the perfect example of a businessman who has his way with business. Undoubtedly, Mukesh has achieved a lot in his field because of his determination, hard work, and willpower.

# Chapter 32:

# *Six Habits of Self-Love*

We can show gratitude to ourselves for our different achievements in many ways. It is something that most people overlook as a waste of time and resources. This is a fallacy. It is high time we develop habits of self-love, to recharge our bodies and minds in preparation for another phase of achievements.

Here are six habits of self-love:

### 1. Treating Yourself

It is showing gratitude to yourself by way of satisfying your deepest desires instead of waiting for someone else to do it for you. Take the personal initiative to go shopping and buy that designer suit or dress you have been wanting so badly. Do not wait for someone else to do it for you while you are capable.

Take that much-needed vacation and a break from work to be with your family. Spend time with the people you love and cherish every moment because, in this fast-moving world, the future is uncertain. Secure your happiness lest you drown in depression. The best person to take care of your interests is yourself.

Who will take you out for swimming or outing to those posh hotels if you do not initiate it? Self-love begins when you realize your worth and do not allow anyone else to bring it down.

## 2. Celebrate Your Victories

Take advantage of every opportunity to celebrate your wins, no matter how small. A habit of self-love is to celebrate your achievements and ignore voices that discourage you. Nothing should muffle you from shouting your victories to the world. The testimony of your victory will encourage a stranger not to give up in his/her quest.

It is neither pride nor boastfulness. It is congratulating yourself for the wins that you rightfully deserve. How else can you love yourself if you do not appreciate yourself for the milestones you have conquered? Do not shy away from thanking yourself, privately or publicly, because no one else best knows your struggles except yourself.

## 3. Accept Yourself

To begin with, accept your social and economic status because you know the battles you have fought. Self-acceptance is an underrated form of self-love. Love yourself and accept your shortcomings. When you learn to accept yourself, other people will in turn accept you. They will learn how to accommodate you in the same manner you learned to live with all your imperfections.

Self-loathing dies when you master self-acceptance and self-love. Self-care keeps off self-rejection. You begin seeing your worth and great potential. It is the enemy within that is responsible for the fall of great empires.

The enemy within is low self-esteem and self-rejection. Accept the things you cannot change and change the things in your ability. Do not be hard on yourself because a journey of a thousand miles begins with a single step.

## 4. Practice Forgiveness

Forgiveness is a strong act. When you forgive those who wrong you, you let go of unnecessary baggage. It is unhealthy to live with a heart full of hate (pun intended). Forgiveness does not mean that you have allowed other people to wrong you repetitively. It means you have outgrown their wrong acts and you no longer allow their inconsiderate acts to affect you. Forgiveness benefits the forgiver more than the forgiven. It heals the heart from any hurt caused. It is the best form of self-care yet difficult at the same time. Forgiveness is a gradual process initiated by the bigger person in any conflict. Practicing self-care is by recognizing the importance of turning a new leaf and staying free from shackles of grudges and bitterness.

Unforgiveness builds bitterness and vengeance. It finally clouds your judgment and you become irrational. Choosing forgiveness is a vote on self-care.

## 5. Choose Your Associates Wisely

Associate with progressive people. Show me your friends and I will tell you the kind of person you are. Your friends have the potential to either build or destroy your appreciation of self-worth. They will trim your excesses and supplement your deficiencies. A cadre of professionals tends to share several traits.

Self-care involves taking care of your mental state and being selective of who you let into your personal space. It supersedes all other interests.

### 6. Engaging In Hobbies

Hobbies are the activities we do during our free time to relax our minds and bond with our friends. When doing these hobbies we are at ease and free from pressures of whatever form. We need to take a break from our daily work routine from time to time and do other social activities.

Hobbies are essential to explore other interests and rejuvenate our psyche and morale. Self-love places your interests and well-being above everything else. There is a thin line between it and selfishness, but it is not the latter.

These six habits of self-love will ensure you have peace and sobriety of mind to make progressive decisions.

## Chapter 33:

# 6 Concerning Effects of Mood On Your Life

*By definition, mood is the predominant state of our mind which clouds over all the other emotions and judgements. Our mood represents the surface-level condition of our emotional self.*

Mood is very versatile and sensitive. Subtle changes in our surroundings or even changes in our thoughts directly affect mood. And consequently, our mood, being the leader of our mental state, affects us, as a whole—even impacting our life directly.

Take notes of these following points so that you can overpower your mood and take complete control of your life.

Here Are 6 Ways How Changes In Your Mood Can Impact Your Life:

## 1. Mood On Your Judgement and Decision-Making

Humans are the most rational beings—fitted with the most advanced neural organ, the brain. Scientists say that our brain is capable of making one thousand trillion logical operations per second and yet still, we humans are never surprised to make the stupidest of judgements in real life.

Well, along with such an enormous 'Logical reasoning' capacity, our brains also come with an emotional center and that is where mood comes in to crash all logic. Most of the decisions we make are emotional, not logical. Since our emotions are steered by mood, it is no surprise that we often make irrational decisions out of emotional impulses.

But again, there are also some instances where mood-dictated decisions reap better outcomes compared to a logical decision. That's just life.

## 2. Mood Affects Your Mental Health

While our mood is a holistic reflection of our mental state caused by various external and internal factors, it is also a fact that our mood can be the outcome of some harboring mental illness. Both high degree of euphoria and depression can be an indication of mood disorder—just on two opposite ends of the spectrum.

There is no specific cause behind it except that it is a culmination of prolonged mood irregularities. And mood irregularities may come from anywhere i.e. worrying, quarrelling, drug abuse, period/puberty, hormonal changes etc. If such mood irregularity persists untreated, it may deteriorate your overall mental health and result in more serious conditions. So, consider monitoring your mood changes often.

## 3. Correlation Between Mood and Physical Well-Being

We have heard the proverb that goes, "A healthy body is a healthy mind". Basically, our body and mind function together. So, if your body is in a healthy state, your mind will reflect it by functioning properly as well. If on the other hand your body is not in a healthy state, due to lack of proper nutrition, sleep, and exercise, then your mind will become weak as well. Yes, according to research, having a persistent bad mood can lead to chronic stress which gradually creates hormonal imbalance in your body and thus, diseases like diabetes, hypertension, stroke etc. may arise in your body. Negative moods can also make you go age faster than usual. So having a cheerful mood not only keeps you happy but also fuels your body and keeps you young. Aim to keep your body in tip top condition to nourish the mind as well.

## 4. Effect Of Your Mood On Others

This is obvious, right? You wouldn't smile back at your significant other after you have lost your wallet, spilled hot coffee all over yourself and missed the only bus to your job interview.

Your mood overshadows how you behave with others. The only way to break out of this would be to meditate and achieve control over your emotional volatility—believe that whatever happened, happened for a reason. Your sully mood doesn't warrant being hostile with others. Instead, talk to people who want the best of you. Express your griefs.

## 5. Mood As A Catalyst In Your Productivity

Tech giants like Google, Apple, Microsoft all have certain 'play areas' for the employees to go and play different games. It is there to remove mental stress of the employees because mood is an essential factor in determining your productivity at work-place. According to experts, people with a negative mood are 10% less productive in their work than those who are in a positive mood. This correlation between mood and productivity is an important thing to be concerned about.

## 6. Mood Change Your Perspective

Everyone has their own point of view. Perspectives of people vary from individual to individual and similarly, it varies depending on the mood of an individual. On a bad day, even your favorite Starbucks drink would feel tasteless. It doesn't mean that they made a bad drink—it means that you're not in the mood of enjoying its taste. So, how you perceive things and people is greatly affected by your mindset. Pro-tip: Don't throw judgement over someone or something carrying a bad mood. You'll regret it later and think "I totally misread this".

## Final Thoughts

Our mood has plenty of implications on our life. Though our mood is an external representation of our overall mental state, it has its effect on very miniscule aspects of our life to large and macroscopic levels. In the long run, our mood alone can be held responsible for what we have done our whole life—the choices we've made. Though it is really difficult to control our mood, we can always try. Meditating may be one of the possible ways to have our mood on the noose. Because no matter what happens, you wouldn't want your whole life to be an outcome of your emotional impulses would you?

# Chapter 34:

# 9 Habits of Highly Successful People

*Success comes to people who deserve it.* I bet you have heard this statement quite a few times, right? So, what does it mean exactly? Does it mean that you are either born worthy or unworthy of success? Absolutely not. Everyone is born worthy, but the one thing that makes some people successful is their winning habits and their commitment to these habits.

Today, we will learn how to master ten simple habits and behaviors that will help you become successful.

## 1. Be an Avid Learner

If you didn't know, almost all of the most successful people in the world are avid learners. So, do not shy away from opportunities when it comes to learning. Wake up each day and look forward to learning new things, and in no time, I bet you will experience how enriching it really is. Also, learning new things has the effect of revitalizing a person. So, if you want to have more knowledge to kickstart your journey in the right direction, here are some things that you can do - make sure to read, even if it is just a page or two, daily. It could be anything that interests you. I personally love reading self-help books. If you are not that much of a reader, you can even listen to a podcast, watch an informative video, or sign up for a course. Choose what piques your interest, and just dive into it!

## 2. Failure is the Pillar of Success

Most people are afraid to delve into something new, start a new chapter of their lives, and chase after their dreams – all because they are scared to fail. If you are one of those people who are scared to fail, well, don't be! Because what failure actually does is prepares you to achieve your dream. It just makes sure that you are able to handle the success when you finally have it. So when you accept that failure is an inevitable part of your journey, you will be able to plan the right course of action to tackle it instead of just being too scared to move forward. Successful people are never scared of failure; They just turn it around by seeing it as an opportunity to learn.

## 3. Get Up Early

I bet you have heard this a couple of thousand times already! But whoever told you so was not lying. Almost all successful individuals are early risers! They say that starting the morning right ensures a fruitful day ahead. It is true! Think about it, on the day you get up early, you feel a boost of productivity as compared to when you wake up late and have to struggle against the clock. You will have plenty of time and a good mood to go through the rest of the day which will give you better outcomes. All you have to do is set up a bedtime reminder. This is going to make sure that you enough rest to get up in the morning instead of snoozing your alarm on repeat! Not a morning person? Don't worry. I have got you covered! Start slow and set the alarm 15 minutes before when you usually wake up. It doesn't sound like much, eh? But trust me, you will be motivated to wake up earlier when you see how much difference 15 minutes can make to your day.

## 4. Have Your Own Morning Ritual

Morning rituals are the most common habit among achievers. It will pump you up to go through the day with a bang! You just have to make a routine for yourself and make sure to follow it every day. You can take inspiration from the morning routines of people you look up to but remember it has to benefit you. So you might be wondering, *What do I include in the ritual?* I would suggest you make your bed first thing in the morning. This might not sound as great a deal, but hey, it is a tested and approved method to boost your productivity. It is even implemented in the military. Doing this will motivate you as you get a sense of achievement as you have completed a task as soon as you woke up. After that, it could be anything that will encourage you, such as a walk, a workout session, reading, journaling, or meditating.

## 5. Stop Procrastinating

From delaying one task to not keeping up with your deadlines, procrastination becomes a deadly habit. It becomes almost unstoppable! Did you know, most people fail to achieve their dreams even if they have the potential just because of procrastination? Well, they do. And you might not want to become one of them. They say, "Old habits die hard," true, but they do die if you want them to. Procrastination has to be the hardest thing we have to deal with, even though we hey created it in the first place. Trust me, I speak from experience!

So what do you do to stop this? Break your task into small bite-sized pieces. Sometimes, it is just the heaviness of the task that keeps us from doing it. Take breaks in between to keep yourself motivated.

Another thing that you can do is the "minute rule." Divide your tasks by how much time they take. The tasks that take less than 5 minutes, you do it right then. Then you can bigger tasks into small time frames and complete them. Make sure you do not get too lost in the breaks, though!

## 6. Set Goals

I cannot even begin to tell you how effective goal setting is. A goal gives you the right direction and motivation. It also gives you a sense of urgency to do a task that is going to just take your productivity level from 0 to 10 in no time!

So how do you set goals? Simple. Think about the goals you want to achieve and write them down. But make sure that you set realistic goals. If you find it difficult, don't worry. Start small and slow. Start by making a to-do list for the day. You will find out soo that the satisfaction in ticking those off your list is unbelievable. It will also drive you to tick more of them off!

## 7. Make Your Health a Priority

Health is Wealth. Yes, it is a fact! When you give your body the right things and make it a priority, it gives you back by keeping you and your mind healthy. I bet you've heard the saying "You are what you eat," and by "eat," it does not simply mean to chew and swallow! It also means that you need to feed your body, soul, and mind with things you want them to be like. Read, listen, learn, and eat healthy. You could set a goal to eat clean for the week. Or workout at least for 10 minutes. And see for yourself how it gives you the energy to smash those goals you've been holding off! Also, great news – you can have cheat days once a week!

## 8. Plan Your Day the Night Before

"When you fail to plan, you plan to fail." People who succeed in life are not by mere coincidence or luck. It is the result of detailed, focused planning. So, you need to start planning your way to success too. Before you sleep tonight, ask yourself, *What is the most important thing that I have to do tomorrow?* Plan what assignments, meetings, or classes you have to complete. Planning ahead will not only make you organized and ready, it also highly increases your chances to succeed. So, don't forget to plan your day tonight!

## 9. Master the Habit Loop

Behavioral expert, BJ Fogg, explains that habits are formed around three elements: Cue, Routine, and Reward. Cue is the initial desire that motivates your behavior. Routine is the action you take. And the reward is the pleasure you gain after completion. So why am I telling you all of this? Because this habit loop is how we are wired. It is what motivates us. We seek pleasure and avoid pain. And you can use this loop to your advantage! Let's say you want to finish an assignment. Think of the reason why you want to. Maybe you don't want to fall behind someone or want to impress someone. It could be anything! Now time for you to set your rewards. It could be eating a slice of cheesecake or watching an episode of your favorite series after you've finished. Rewards motivate you when you slack off. Play around until you find a combination that works best for you. You will also need a cue; it could be anything like a notification on your phone, an email, or simply your desire. You can set a cue yourself by creating a reminder.

Habits are what make a man. I hope you follow these habits and start your journey the right way to becoming successful in life.

# Chapter 35:

# The High Cost of Good Intentions

Who has not experienced this before: We have been hurt and the person hurting us exclaims in a mixture of surprise and justification that they only meant well! The invocation of the good intention seems to them like an absolution of their responsibility for their action (or inaction) and thus our pain. Having worked as a psychotherapist for many years now with people on the receiving end of all kinds of well intentions (of parents, partners, siblings, classmates, teachers, religious leaders), it is clear to me that this not a sufficient ingredient for good outcome. Really, and I mean here even the truly well intentioned efforts of some parents have at times caused havoc on the lives of their children, that it is heart wrenching to behold, how all sides have lost and suffered in these situations. Why is this so?

It seems that the good intentions may give some a sense of having fulfilled their aim already, thus preventing them to move to action. Like the good intention to ourselves to stop some bad habit of ours and paradoxically the more honest the intention meant at the time the more problematic it may turn out: it thus can better fulfill the very function of calming our worries and anxieties or doubts of being a bad parent, partner or person. Thus good intentions can prove to ourselves that we are not the bad person we may fear we are. To give an example I am very familiar with is procrastinating to study for an exam by repeatedly telling myself, very seriously, that I am going to study "for real" first thing tomorrow, thus feeling at ease today and therefore being able to continue with my not-studying at that very moment, only to have the same pattern repeated the next day. It is the same pattern I see with people struggling with major dependency issues (of any substance and their often futile change efforts), who often will profess with great sincerity that they will stop. It calms them, and often their very afflicted family members as all can sense the honesty of the intent, but thus taking away the force that the suffering provides that is needed to overcome the problem. Good intentions thus can prevent action by removing the psychological motivation that is created by the normal self-doubt, concern about the future (exam, financial situation, you name it ...) or suffering that some undesired state creates, and thus turn against us or the people around us. Then there is the situation where we do move to action but it fails to meet the need of the recipient. I think this is captured well in the bible when Jesus talks about the ones on the right who have feed him when he was hungry, gave drink when he was thirsty. The gift matches the actual need of the recipient. But at times we give water when the person is hungry. This is especially confusing because the receiver may even feel an obligation to be thankful as the other went through the effort of bringing him a gift (albeit one he does not need)! I am not sure if it is possible to capture all the reasons this goes awry (still assuming truly good intentions), but what seems relevant is that the feedback about this mismatch does not reach the giver, for one because the recipient out of the above mentioned conflict does not give it. The second is that the giver will not hear or accept the signs and or direct feedback of the recipient. Why, because he meant well, which is sufficient in their minds to prove they are not the enemy and thus they can discount the other. This is where tragedies start.

## Chapter 36:

# Happy People Don't Sweat the Small Stuff.

Stress follows a peculiar principle: when life hits us with big crises—the death of a loved one or a job loss—we somehow find the inner strength to endure these upheavals in due course. It's the little things that drive us insane day after day—traffic congestion, awful service at a restaurant, an overbearing coworker taking credit for your work, meddling in-laws, for example.

It's all too easy to get caught up in the many irritations of life. We overdramatize and overreact to life's myriad tribulations. Under the direct influence of anguish, our minds are bewildered, and we feel disoriented. This creates stress, which makes the problems more difficult to deal with.

The central thesis of psychotherapist Richard Carlson's bestselling *Doesn't Sweat The Small Stuff... And It's All Small Stuff* (1997) is this: to deal with angst or anger, we need not some upbeat self-help prescriptions for changing ourselves, but simply a measure of perspective.

Perspective helps us understand that there's an art to understand what we should let go of and what we should concern ourselves with. It is important to focus our efforts on the important stuff and not waste time on insignificant and incidental things.

I've previously written about my favorite 5-5-5 technique for gaining perspective and guarding myself against anger erupting: I remove myself from the offending environment and contemplate if whatever I'm getting worked up over is of importance. I ask myself, "Will this matter in 5 days? Will this matter in 5 months? Will this matter in 5 years?"

Carlson stresses that there's always a vantage point from which even the biggest stressor can be effectively dealt with. The challenge is to keep making that shift in perspective. When we achieve that "wise-person-in-me" perspective, our problems seem more controllable and our lives more peaceful.

Carlson's prescriptions aren't uncommon—we can learn to be more patient, compassionate, generous, grateful, and kind, all of which will improve the way we feel about ourselves and how other people feel when they are around us.

Some of Carlson's 100 recommendations are trite and banal—for example, "make peace with imperfection," "think of your problems as potential teachers," "remember that when you die, your 'in-basket' won't be empty," and "do one thing at a time." Others are more informative:

- Let others have the glory

- Let others be "right" most of the time
- Become aware of your moods, and don't allow yourself to be fooled by the low ones
- Look beyond behavior
- Every day, tell at least one person something you like, admire, or appreciate about them.
- Argue for your limitations, and they're yours
- Resist the urge to criticize
- Read articles and books with entirely different points of view from your own and try to learn something.